KINGFISHER
POCKET BOOK OF
AIRCRAFT

Roy Braybrook

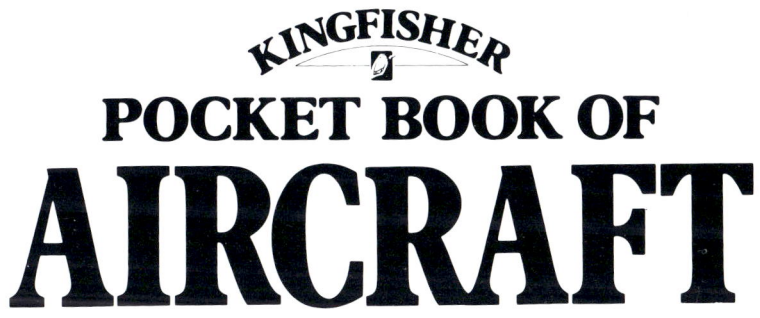

Kingfisher Books

First Published in 1985 by Kingfisher
Books Limited, Elsley Court,
20–22 Great Titchfield Street,
London W1P 7AD
A Grisewood & Dempsey Company

BRITISH LIBRARY CATALOGUING
IN PUBLICATION DATA
Braybrook, Roy
    Aircraft. – (Kingfisher pocket books)
    1. Aeronautics – Juvenile literature
    I. Title
    629.133   TL547

    ISBN 0–86272–144–X

Edited by Kate Hayden
Cover design by Pinpoint Design
Company
Illustrations by Brian Knight, Janos
Marffy, Jack Pelling, Michael Roffe,
Michael Saunders, Glenn Steward,
Michael Trim.
Printed and bound in Portugal by Printer Portuguesa - Sintra

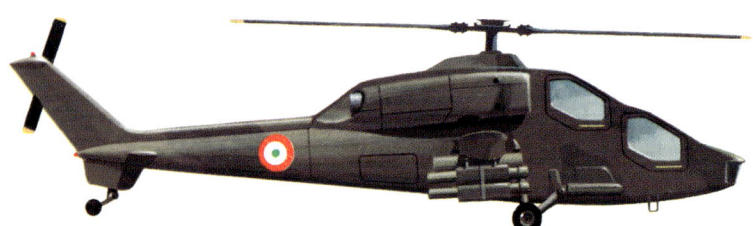

Contents

Introduction

Anyone who has visited an airshow will have been excited and intrigued by the sight, the sound and the speed of the aircraft on display. And yet aviation is far more than a mere spectacle. Powered flight as we know it today is less than a century old, but in that short time it has transformed our lives. Many people alive today in the Concorde era of supersonic travel were born before the Wright brothers made their first powered flight in 1903!

Until the 1930s, aviation was still a dangerous business and far too expensive for the average man, even in the most prosperous countries. In the early decades of air travel, piston engines were notoriously unreliable, and aircraft lacked the instruments and the radio aids to fly safely at night or in bad conditions. World War II brought a wide range of developments in both civil and military aviation. In the late 1950s, jet airliners brought high-speed travel within the reach of millions. This enabled some people to travel to distant countries. Journeys that once took weeks now only took a few hours.

Air travel also revolutionized international trade. Urgent cargo could be flown anywhere in the world in less than a day. A salesman could visit clients abroad, demonstrate his wares on the spot, and fly home with the contract signed.

◀ Air travel of the past. The 'Bristol' Pullman was the first large airliner. It could seat up to 14 passengers.

▼ Air travel of the future. The Airbus A320 is expected to make its first commercial flight in 1988.

It is sad but true that aviation moves ahead more quickly in times of war than in peacetime. When the survival of a nation is at stake, the costs of new developments are much more acceptable. In times of peace, the cost of new military developments has to be weighed against the funding of new hospitals, roads or housing – things for which clear and immediate needs exist. So in peace the lead in aviation development is often taken by the commercial side of the industry. When progress depends on advances in the airliner field, it tends to take place in a series of small, safe steps, because the manufacturers cannot afford to take expensive risks. The Concorde supersonic transport is an exception to this rule, but in that case all the initial costs were borne by the British and French governments.

As one of the most important developments of the 20th century, aviation is well worth studying. Many aviation enthusiasts become 'plane-spotters', learning how to recognize the most obscure aircraft. Unfortunately, spotters have to remember that in some countries an interest in aircraft is strongly discouraged, and the recording of serial numbers and the taking of photographs is regarded as espionage. The only equipment the spotter really needs is a notebook, but binoculars (of at least 8× magnification) are a great asset.

The Rise of Aviation

For thousands of years men and women were bound to the Earth by gravity. They observed but failed to imitate the effortless flight of birds. Even some of the simplest creatures can fly. Many tiny insects can move at up to 8 km/h (5 mph), a remarkable speed for their size. Dragonflies can wing their way through the air at 24 km/h (15 mph). Many birds can fly at twice this speed, and racing pigeons can reach 144 km/h (90 mph). This wonderful freedom of flight was beyond the power of men and women.

But if people lacked the natural ability to fly, they certainly had no lack of ingenuity. They invented the wheel, which enabled them to travel quickly and move heavy loads on land. They made boats that could support them on water and allowed them to move over the surface of the sea. Clearly it was only a question of time before people found a way of supporting themselves in the air.

Manned flight represents the third great advance in our ability to move from one place to another. Whereas the fourth advance – space travel – was achieved by tremendous power alone, aviation was achieved by observing natural phenomena and by inventiveness.

First Flying Machines

The first man-made flying objects were probably Chinese kites, made possible by the invention of lightweight paper in the second century AD. Although generally made as toys, they put to use some of the basic properties of more serious flying machines. For example, the flying ability of the kite depended on its weight and surface area, and the speed of the relative wind. It also depended on stability, provided by its long tail.

Unfortunately people were unable to work out from the tethered kite how much wing area would be required to support the weight of a man or woman. Most drawings that survive of early schemes for wingborne flight show men equipped with feathered wings that were far too small. The wings were generally attached too high on the man's back to support him in a horizontal position, and there was no tail to provide stability. Generations of winged

◀ **Kay Ka'us, king of Persia,** was said to have flown in a throne supported by geese. This 15th-century miniature shows him shooting at an angel from his flying vessel.

'tower-jumpers' died or injured themselves pointlessly. If people had used much larger, lightweight wings and attached them around the waist rather than to the shoulders, people might have attained brief gliding flight many years earlier than they did.

The well-known legend about Daedalus and Icarus who flew with wings made from birds' feathers was a false lead. In the story Icarus fell into the sea when the sun melted the wax adhesive that attached his wings. People were right to try to imitate the gliding flight of birds, with the wings fixed in one position. Where they were mistaken was in trying to copy the way birds moved forward by flapping their wings. People do not have the muscles that enable birds to propel themselves in this way, the ones that cause the bulging chest of the racing pigeon.

Time passed, and people continued to struggle with the problem of overcoming gravity, but to little avail. Around 1500 AD Leonardo da Vinci sketched an ornithopter – a flying rotating screw-wing machine, but the even older Chinese 'flying-top' toy and the aborigine's boomerang were probably closer to the modern helicopter.

▲ **Leonardo's design** for a helicopter dates from the mid-16th century.

Hot Air and Hydrogen

Imitation of birds and winged insects was not the only way in which people tried to fly. Another method came from the observation that the hot gases produced by a fire rise through the cooler air and that any gas will try to rise if it is less dense than the surrounding air. If placed in a lightweight container, a low-density gas can produce a lifting force, acting against gravity. If the container is large enough, and the gas density low enough, it can even support a person.

In 1670 a Jesuit priest, Francesco de Lana-Terzi, proposed a 'flying-boat' propelled by a sail, and supported by four copper spheres from which all the air had been pumped. To prevent the spheres from collapsing, the copper needed to be fairly thick, but this made the spheres far too heavy. What was needed was not a vacuum, but a low density gas at about the same pressure as the surrounding air. (Modern helium balloons are based on this principle.) In 1709 another Jesuit, Laurenço da Gusmão, displayed an aircraft named the *Passarola* (Great Bird). It had bat-like wings, a type of parachute over the body and a tail for stability. It may have flown in model form, as a glider. A later model

13

demonstrated by da Gusmão rose from the ground when a small fire was lit under the parachute.

Surprisingly, little notice seems to have been taken of this important event at the time. The Montgolfier brothers' hot air balloon came much later in the century. They began their experiments at home, trapping hot air from a burning fire in a silk bag, which promptly rose to the ceiling. In June 1783 they tested a full-scale (though unmanned) balloon some 11·6 metres (38 feet)

The Montgolfiers' hot air balloon

Blanchard and Jeffries' hydrogen-filled balloon

in diameter, which reached a height of about 1800 metres (6000 feet). Three weeks later they sent up an even bigger balloon, carrying a sheep, a cockerel and a duck. Later that year a young French doctor, Jean-François Pilâtre de Rozier, became the first person to fly in a hot air balloon (which was tied to the ground).

The first great milestone in recorded manned flight came on 21 November 1783, when de Rozier and the Marquis d'Arlandes became the first people to fly in a balloon that was not tethered to the ground. They flew 9 kilometres (5·6 miles) across Paris in a Montgolfier balloon and reached a height of about 900 metres (3000 feet). The direction of motion was still dictated by the wind, but air travel had begun! On 1 December two balloon flights were made by another Frenchman, Professor J. A. C. Charles, using hydrogen instead of hot air. On the first flight it carried two men

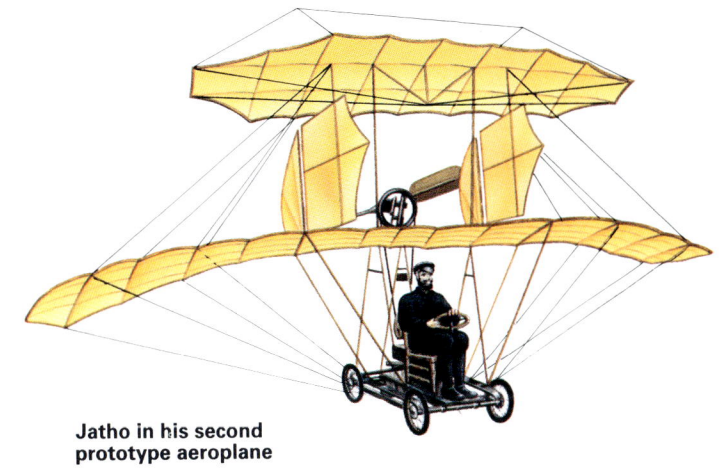

Jatho in his second prototype aeroplane

and covered a distance of 43 kilometres (27 miles) in two hours. On the second, with only one man on board, it reached an altitude of around 3000 metres (10,000 feet). In terms of commercial and military developments, this type of balloon was to be of far greater importance than the hot air variety. But hydrogen is highly flammable, which is why it has been replaced by helium, whenever possible.

Gliders

The successful development of man-carrying balloons encouraged work on aircraft supported by wings. The next step would be to develop an aircraft which would allow the operator to choose the direction in which he was to travel, freeing him from the dictates of the winds. In England Sir George Cayley invented several of the features needed for a practical aeroplane. In 1804 he flew a model glider with a kite-like wing, an adjustable tail, and a lead weight to move its centre of gravity. Five years later Cayley had produced a full-scale glider, but it was tested unmanned with ballast. No further experiments appear to have been made until 1853, when a Cayley glider with fixed controls was used to fly his coachman across a valley, probably the first manned glide by a stable aircraft. The coachman did not relish the role of test-pilot, and left to find less hazardous employment.

Cayley contributed a great deal more to aircraft development. Apart from building a stable glider, he had emphasized the value of streamlining and wing camber – slight convexity of the upper wing surface which gives greater lifting power. He also proposed wire-braced biplane and triplane wings for minimum weight and maximum rigidity. It was Cayley who invented wing dihedral. This means that the tips of the wings are higher than the wing roots, and it is a design feature which makes aircraft more stable. Another important English pioneer was Horatio Phillips. He discovered that the best form of wing section was not only cambered but also thick, with a rounded leading edge (at the front) and a sharp trailing edge (at the back). The shape of an aeroplane's wing, known as *aerofoil*, is based on complex mathematical calculations. Expressed in simple terms, lift is achieved by the shape of the wing and by angling it slightly upward. This angle is called the *angle of attack*.

THE AEROFOIL

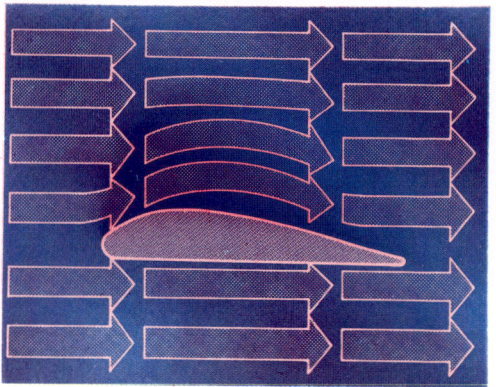

The shape of an aircraft's wing is called an aerofoil; it is specially shaped to produce lift and support the aircraft.
   The air passing over the top surfaces flows faster than the air passing beneath because it has further to go. As a result the air pressure above the wing is less than the air pressure below, producing lift to counterbalance the aircraft's weight.

Pioneers of Powered Flight

Once the fundamental ideas of aircraft design were established, the next step was to produce stable, controllable gliders. Powered, sustained flight would then come with the gradual development of lightweight engines.

Towards the end of the 19th century there was a succession of experiments with full-scale aircraft and models, the latter using all kinds of power, including elastic, clockwork, compressed air and steam. One of the most interesting of the many powered devices that hopped briefly off the ground was the *Eole* built by Clement Ader of France. On 9 October 1890 it covered a distance of about 45 metres (150 feet) in the air. Some historians regard it as the first man-carrying aircraft to leave level ground under its own power.

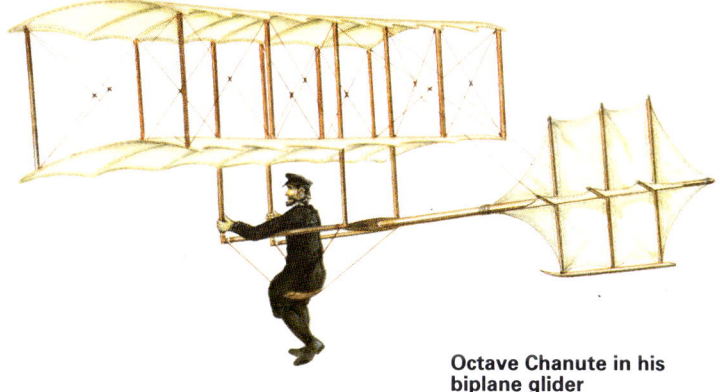

Octave Chanute in his biplane glider

At that time, none of the engines available were powerful enough to support the weight of a manned aircraft for any length of time. The people who were laying the real groundwork for future aircraft were the men building and flying gliders. It was they who were learning the fundamentals of flight – how to build comparatively safe, strong structures, wings with good lifting behaviour, aircraft with adequate stability and effective controls.

One of the leaders in the gliding field was Germany's Otto Lilienthal, who might well have achieved powered flight late in 1896, but was killed in August that year. Other pioneers were Percy Pilcher in England and Octave Chanute in the US. While such men were laying the foundations of aerodynamics and structural practice, others were working on developing engines.

Daimler produced the first liquid-fuel engine in 1880, and shortly afterwards the Australian, Lawrence Hargrave invented the rotary engine that was to play a major role in the first decades of aviation. Hargrave also invented the box-kite, which formed the basis for many early aircraft structures.

▲ **A Wright biplane** at Kitty Hawk

The Wrights

The Wright brothers arrived on the scene at a stage when man-carrying gliders were performing quite reliably and when engines had been developed which could give enough power without too much weight. The brothers were inspired by the example of Lilienthal and other gliding pioneers. They also had the right blend of theory and practical testing to bring powered, manned flight to reality.

The Wrights began in 1899 with an unmanned glider, flown like a kite at the end of a cable. They built their own wind-tunnel and in it developed their own wing sections. Between 1902 and 1903 they made hundreds of gliding flights with their No 3 aircraft. They improved their control system to give co-ordinated turns, using rudder in combination with wing-warping. A horizontal foreplane was devised to pitch the nose of the plane up or down. This tail-first arrangement is known as a canard.

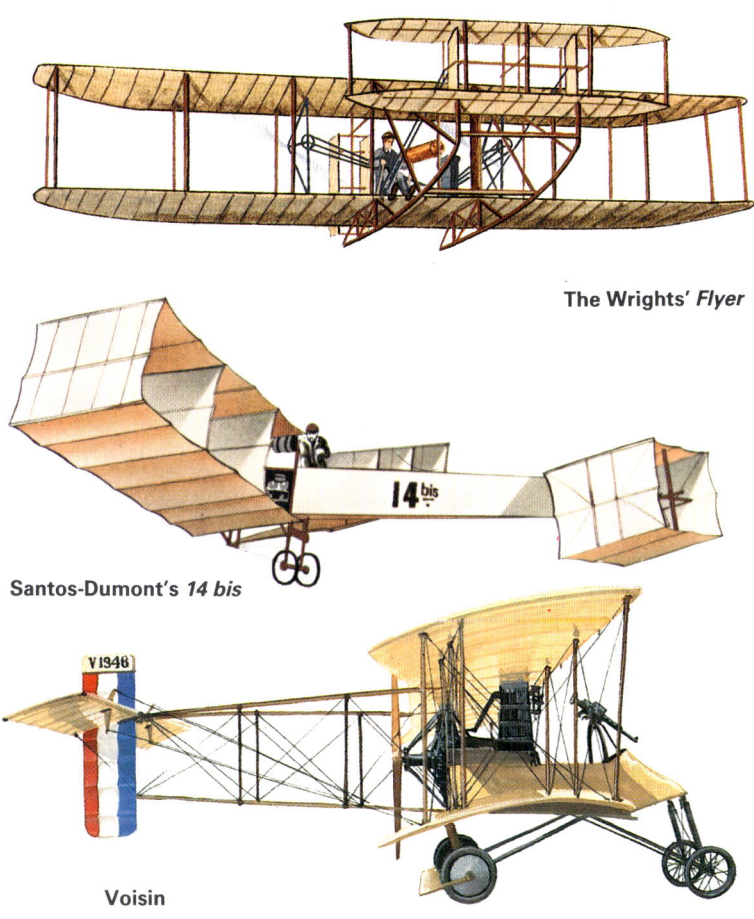

The Wrights' *Flyer*

Santos-Dumont's *14 bis*

Voisin

When they turned their attention to powered aircraft, the Wrights had to scale up their best glider, to allow for the extra weight of the engine. The resulting Wright 'Flyer' of 1903 was fitted with a four-cylinder engine they had designed and built. It produced a mere 12 hp, but this was just enough for the purpose. On 17 December 1903 at Kill Devil Hill, Kitty Hawk, on the North Carolina coast, Orville Wright made what is generally recognized as the first sustained flight in a fully-controlled heavier-than-air machine operating under its own power.

There were other aviators who believed that the title awarded to the Wrights was rightfully theirs. One of these was Germany's Karl Jatho who flew near Hanover on 18 August 1903. What gives special significance to the Wrights was partly the size of the 'Flyer' hops, which demonstrated the aircraft's stability. On that first flight it covered 36·6 metres (120 feet) and was 12 seconds in the air, but the best that day lasted for 59 seconds over a distance of 259 metres (852 feet).

The Wright brothers also stood out from their fellow-pioneers in that they went on to develop their aircraft, and to demonstrate them very convincingly both in America and in Europe. They had put powered flight on a sound basis, and their success eventually encouraged others to devote their energies and money to the cause of aircraft development. It was still several years, however, before the importance of their achievement was fully appreciated.

Aviators on the Move
The first flight of significance in Europe came on 23 October 1906. The pioneer in this case was a Brazilian, Alberto Santos-Dumont, and his aircraft ('14 *bis*') combined the canard layout with the box-kite structure developed by Hargrave. By 1908 Henry Farman (an Englishman living in France) had won a prize for flying his Voisin biplane around a 1500 metre (4900 feet) circuit. The world's first air races took place at Rheims in France in August 1909. Around 250,000 people went to watch.

Sikorsky's *Le Grand*

One event that had fired the imagination of the public was Louis Blériot's flight across the Channel on 25 July that year. Piloting a Blériot IX monoplane, fitted with a three-cylinder air-cooled 24 hp Anzani engine, he covered the 37·5 kilometres (23·5 miles) from Calais to Dover in just over 36 minutes. Suddenly, Britain was no longer as remote from Continental Europe as it had been. It was possible to foresee a time when the aeroplane would provide high-speed links across the Channel. Travel time between British and Continental cities would eventually be only a fraction of the time taken by train and boat. But this also meant that Britain was no longer as secure from attack and invasion as it had been.

▲ **Louis Blériot** prepares to leave France on his cross-channel trip of 1909.

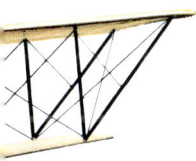

The years just before World War I saw many other 'firsts', though in most cases these events had no immediate practical significance. The first recorded untethered flight by a rotary-wing aircraft was made by France's Paul Cornu, with a free hover on 13 November 1907. The first powered flight from water was performed by Henri Fabre on 28 March 1910, though the first practical seaplane is generally attributed to America's Glenn Curtiss, with a first flight on 26 January 1911.

Although the name of Sikorsky is now associated with helicopters, in the early days it was linked with the largest aeroplanes. In 1912 Igor Sikorsky, who then lived in Russia, began construction of the *Grand*, a four-engined biplane with a span of 28 metres (92 feet) and a weight of about 4000 kg (8800 lb). It first flew on 13

May 1913, and was followed by the even larger *Ilia Mourometz*. At the opposite extreme, Armand Deperdussin in France was building small monoplane racers. The first Schneider Trophy race (1913) was won by a Deperdussin on floats, averaging 74 km/h (45·75 mph). In the same year a wheeled version established a speed record of 203 km/h (126·67 mph).

▲ The *'Nulli Secundus'* ('Second to None'),
Britain's first military airship, on show at
Farnborough in 1907.

Putting Aeroplanes to Practical Use
It was natural that, as aeroplanes became more reliable and faster, they should attract the attention of both the military and mail services. Balloons had been used to take messages and VIP passengers out of Paris during the siege of 1870. Tethered balloons had been used for battlefield observation even earlier: as far back as 1793 in France. Count von Zeppelin's first practical airship had flown in 1900 (the first fully controllable airship was produced by Renard and Krebs in 1884) and Germany adopted the Zeppelin series for both military and civil roles. The German Army bought the LZ.3 in 1908, and the series also formed the basis for DELAG, the world's first commercial airline (founded 1909).

The first US Army aeroplane was a two-seat Wright biplane, purchased in 1908 for $25,000. From experience with balloons, the main military interest at that time was in using aeroplanes for reconnaissance, but some thought was given to arming them. In August 1910 Lt. Fickel of the US Army fired a rifle from a Curtiss biplane in flight near New York. A machine gun installation for an aircraft was patented in Germany by Euler that same year, and Voisin showed a machine gun in a two-seat pusher biplane at a Paris exhibition. In January 1911 the first bomb was dropped, from a Wright biplane near San Francisco. Because of the problems of firing a machine gun through a rotating propeller, many early military aircraft were 'pushers', with the engine at the rear of the fuselage. This arrangement put the observer in the nose where he had an excellent field of view. From May 1912 until the outbreak of war the British and French had a ban on monoplanes, due to a series of fatal accidents in this category.

The practical application of aeroplanes was not, however, limited to the military. In February 1911 a Humber biplane was used to carry mail to Allahabad in India. Later in the year, an airmail service was run between Hendon aerodrome and Windsor, to commemorate the coronation of King George V. In 1914 the St Petersburg-Tampa Airboat Line began scheduled passenger services across Tampa Bay, Florida, using the Benoist flying-boat, which could accommodate a pilot and one passenger. A modest start had been made in the practical application of aeroplanes and World War I brought the urgency to accelerate further progress in the air.

▼ **A still from** *Those Magnificent Men in Their Flying Machines*, showing how flimsy early aircraft were.

World War I (1914-1918)

At the outbreak of World War I, military aviation was still in its infancy. The basic problem of installing a machine gun had not yet been solved. High performance from the aircraft meant a tractor arrangement, with the propeller at the front, which restricted the field of fire. In the case of a two-seat reconnaissance aircraft, the pattern was set by Germany's Albatross C.I, which had the observer in the rear cockpit, with a flexibly-mounted gun on a ring-mount.

The single-seat 'fighting scout' was more of a problem. The Bristol Scout C was tested with a Lewis gun angled off to the side, firing outside the propellor, but pilots found this an awkward arrangement. In essence, they wanted to fire in the direction they

▲ **Three of the fighter 'aces'** of World War I.
From left to right: Guynemer (France),
Richthofen (Germany) and Albert Ball
(Britain).

were flying. Raymond Saulnier experimented with an 'interrupter gear' that would allow a machine gun to fire between the rotating propeller blades, but the cartridges tended to hang fire and shoot holes in the blades. He therefore fitted steel deflector plates to the blades and threw away the interrupter gear.

Tested on a Morane L monoplane in front-line operations, the deflector plates worked very well. The Morane shot down five German aircraft in April 1915, but was then forced to land behind enemy lines, and the 'secret weapon' was no longer a secret. Ironically, the deflector plates were no use to the Germans, since they used steel-jacketed bullets (rather than the soft copper jackets of the French *cartouches*), but this French system forced

▲ **A pilot poses** beside his aircraft, an R.E.8

the Germans to develop their own synchronization gear. This was done by a Dutchman, Anthony Fokker, working in Berlin, and based on a patent filed by Franz Schneider in 1913. This system entered service with the Fokker E.I monoplane, and the first 'kill' with a properly synchronized weapon took place on 15 June 1915.

The Battle for Supremacy in the Air
Control of the air over the trenches swung from side to side. The 'Fokker Scourge' lasted well into 1916, when the Allies introduced a new fighter generation. The Sopwith 1½-Strutter was the first British fighter with an interrupter gear. It was followed by the same company's Pup and Triplane, and France's Nieuport 17 and Spad 7. Late in 1916 the air war swung back in Germany's favour, with the advent of the Halberstadt and Albatros D-series biplanes, and the Fokker Dr.I triplane. In the summer of 1917 the Allies hit back with the Sopwith Camel, Bristol Fighter and Spad 13, each of which had the twin-gun armament of the previous German generation, and were better aircraft. The last few months of the war saw one more swing in the battle for air superiority, when Germany introduced the Fokker D.VII in April 1918. Britain's Sopwith Snipe and France's Nieuport 28 arrived too late to play a significant role.

In the course of the war, engines had increased from around 80 hp to 300 hp. Speeds had gone from 112 km/h (70 mph) to 230 km/h (144 mph). Service ceilings had gone from 4000 metres (13,100 ft.) to around 7300 metres (24,000 ft.). Aircraft generally still had wooden structures with fabric covering, but some German fighters

FIGHTER PLANES OF WORLD WAR I

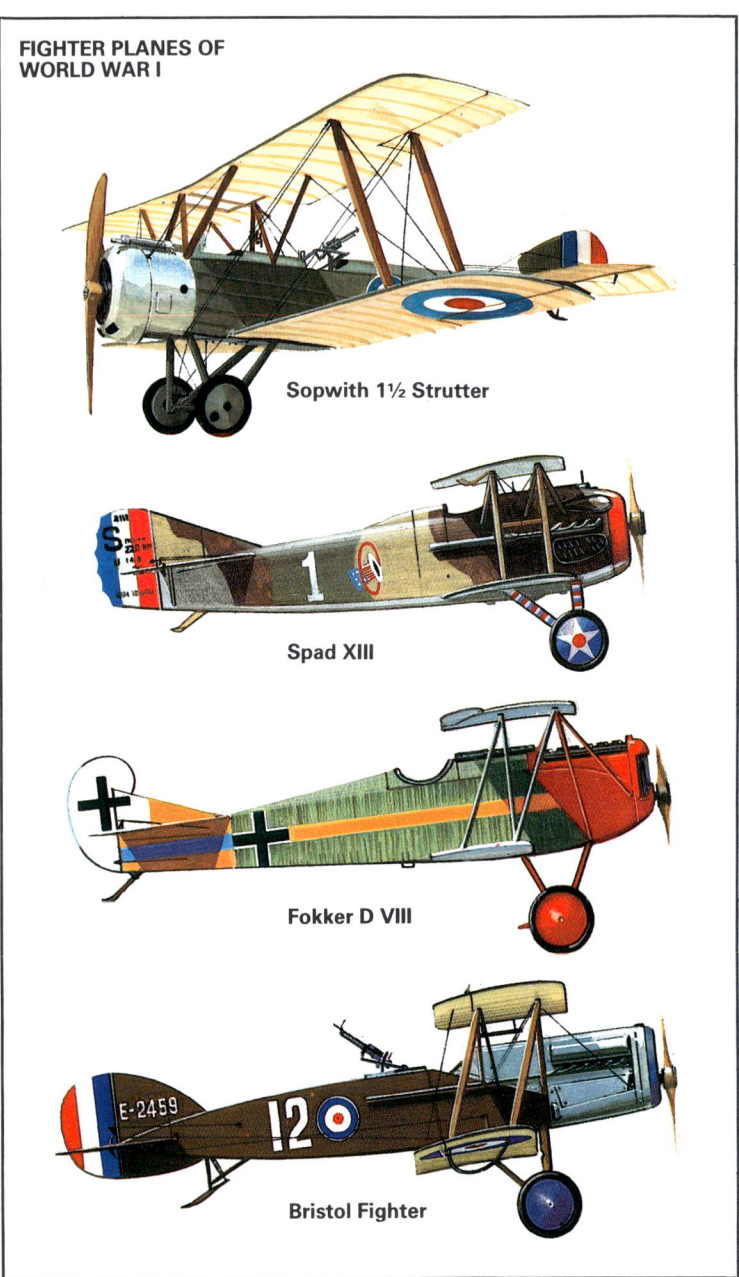

Sopwith 1½ Strutter

Spad XIII

Fokker D VIII

Bristol Fighter

had stressed-skin wooden fuselages, and in 1915 Junkers had built the first all-metal unbraced monoplane. Some two-seaters had radios, but they could communicate only by Morse-code telegraphy, not speech. Parachutes (first demonstrated from an aircraft in 1912) were not used until 1918, and then only on the German side.

Some of the most effective bombing was performed by Zeppelins, which first raided Antwerp in Belgium in 1914. They made their first attack on the east coast of England in January 1915, and their first on London in August that year. However, by 1916 they were suffering heavy losses due to ground fire and fighters, which were now able to operate at night and had special ammunition to ignite the airship's hydrogen. The Zeppelin was switched to attack shipping in the North Sea, but Sopwith Pups were flown on air defence missions from small decks on early 'carriers'. They could not land on the carriers. Instead they ditched in the sea alongside.

Beginning in 1917, England was raided by heavy bombers, such as the Gotha G.IV, with the even heavier Zeppelin-Staaken R.VI entering service in the following year. The Allies responded with bombers such as the Caproni Ca.33 and the Handley Page 0/100 and 0/400. These were very successful aircraft, though far smaller than the R.VI, which weighed up to 11,460 kg (25,265 lb) and had a span of 42·22 metres (138 ft. 6 in.).

Between the Wars

In the immediate post-war years there was no money for further military developments. Commercial aviation made a slow start, encouraged by some remarkable long-distance flights. In May 1919 the first crossing of the Atlantic was made by a Curtiss NC-4 flying boat, commanded by Lt. Cdr. A. C. Read, flying from Newfoundland to Plymouth via the Azores and Lisbon. The first non-stop crossing was made by Alcock and Brown in a Vickers Vimy in the following month, flying from Newfoundland to Ireland. Later that year another Vimy made the first flight from Britain to Australia. The Junkers F.13, the first all-metal aircraft to enter airline service, also flew that year.

The 1920s saw more technical progress and record flights using a new generation of aircraft. In Spain, Cierva began testing his autogiros, rotary-wing devices in which power is applied to a conventional propeller, rather than the rotor. The years that followed saw many notable 'firsts'.

The 1930s were a time for new military aircraft, as war drew nearer, but great strides were also being taken in commercial aviation. Biplane fighters, such as Britain's Gladiator, Italy's Fiat CR.42, and Russia's Polikarpov I-153 continued to be developed, but monoplanes were taking over. The Boeing P-26 of 1933 was the first all-metal monoplane fighter, but it had a fixed undercarriage, like France's Dewoitine D.500, Japan's Mitsubishi A5M, and the Dutch Fokker D.XXI. The first single-seat low-wing monoplane fighter with a retractable undercarriage was the Polikarpov I-16. This set the pattern for a whole generation of fighters, such as the Messerschmitt Bf 109, which it fought against in the Spanish Civil War. The trend was towards metal construction, enclosed cockpits, high octane fuel, variable-pitch propellers and radio telephony (voice communication).

Meanwhile, a start had been made with aeroplanes for private owners. The DH Moth of 1925 was followed by the Mignet *Pou de Ciel* of 1933, the Klemm monoplane of 1935, and the Piper Cub of 1938. In the field of airliners, the Handley Page HP.42 biplane of 1930 was followed by the DC-1 and Boeing 247 monoplanes in 1933, the DC-2 in 1934 and the famous DC-3 in 1935. The Boeing 307 Stratoliner of 1938 was the world's first pressurized airliner. Flying boats continued to have special attractions in far-flung regions, hence the Sikorsky S-42 Clipper of 1934 and the Short Empire flying boat of 1936.

▼ Sir John Alcock and Sir Arthur Brown
were the first people to fly non-stop across
the Atlantic in 1919.

Technological advances included the Focke-Achgelis helicopter of 1937. But perhaps the most significant event was the first flight of a turbojet aircraft, the Heinkel He 178 on 24 August 1939. Although it was to have little impact on the war that followed, the gas turbine engine was the key to future aviation development.

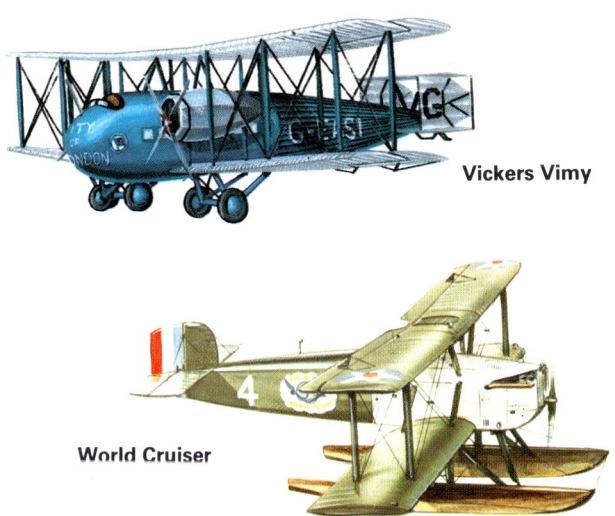

Vickers Vimy

World Cruiser

FAMOUS FIRSTS

1924 Two Douglas World Cruisers fly around the world in six months.
1925 The Ford Tri-Motor 'Tin Goose' makes its first flight. The Schneider Trophy is won for the last time by a bi-plane, a Curtiss R3C-2 averaging 372 km/h (232·5 mph).
1926 Three-engined Fokker FVII is flown over the North Pole.
1927 Lindberg crosses the Atlantic in his Ryan monoplane *Spirit of St Louis*.
1928 Kingsford-Smith crosses the Pacific in a Fokker VII. Passenger services across the North and South Atlantic inaugurated. Services end after the destruction of LZ-129 'Hindenberg' in May 1937.
1929 LZ 127 Graf Zeppelin completes round-the-world trip. Dornier DOX flying boat makes first flight. Germans begin test with rocket-powered glider.
1930 Amy Johnson flies from Britain to Australia in a DH Moth.
1933 Wily Post completes his round-the-world trip in 7 days, 18 hours and 14 minutes.

World War II (1939-1945)

Radar was of vital importance in the war, and in this field Britain had a world lead. It was one of the main factors in the Battle of Britain in the summer of 1940, since it allowed the handful of RAF fighters to be in the right place at the right time. The Supermarine Spitfire and Messerschmitt Bf 109 were technically the most advanced fighters at that time. But the fight was won by the Hawker Hurricane, which, although slightly slower, was very easy to build and repair. It was thus available in far greater numbers than the Spitfire.

Fokke-Wulf FW 190

Reggiane Re 2001

On the RAF side, the Hurricane was soon switched to ground attack, but the Spitfire remained an outstanding fighter (especially at high altitude) throughout the war. At lower levels it was superseded by the Hawker Typhoon and the Tempest. The Messerschmitt Bf 109 had the distinction of being produced in larger numbers than any other aircraft, about 35,000 being built between 1936 and 1945. Italy had chosen to concentrate on biplane fighters, and also lagged behind in engine development. It was only late in the war, using Daimler-Benz engines in monoplane fighters such as the Macchi C205V, that Italy's combat aircraft could compete with those of the Allies.

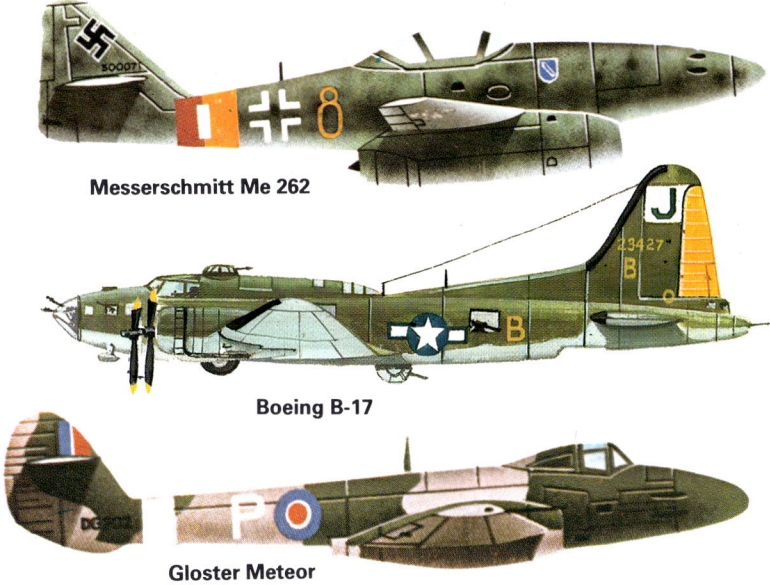

Messerschmitt Me 262

Boeing B-17

Gloster Meteor

The Post-war Years

By the end of the war there were airfields even in the most remote areas, and the need for flying boats had virtually disappeared. America ended the war with good commercial transports. The Douglas DC-4 was developed into the DC-6/DC-7 series, and the Lockheed Constellation into the Super Constellation. Together with the Boeing Stratocruiser, these aircraft dominated the piston-engined airliner market on the late 1940s and 1950s.

As countries recovered from the war, the demand for light aircraft boomed. Companies such as Beech, Cessna and Piper built aircraft by the thousand. The demand for high-speed transportation produced a market for business jets, such as the Gates Learjet and Dassault-Breguet Falcon/Mystère series.

The Rise of the Rotary-Wing
The past 40 years have seen a great increase in the numbers of helicopters; the US Army alone now has over 7000. Rotary-wing aircraft were little used in World War II. It was the Korean War of 1950–53 that really established the helicopter as a practical form of transport, particularly in the rescue role. The introduction of lightweight turbine engines greatly improved their effectiveness.

Mig-15

North American
F-86 Sabre

Wars in Korea and Vietnam

Advances have also been made in combat aircraft. The Korean War saw the first combats between swept-wing jet fighters, the North American F-86 Sabre and the MiG-15. It also witnessed the first large-scale use of in-flight refuelling to move aircraft quickly across the Pacific. The early 1950s saw USAF Strategic Air Command switching from the piston-engined B-36 to the jet-engined, swept-wing Boeing B-47, which from the mid-1950s began to be supplemented by the massive B-52 Stratofortress (later used in Vietnam).

The Korean War led to a generation of relatively lightweight Mach 2 fighters (Lockheed F-104 Starfighter, Dassault Mirage III and MiG-21) in the 1960s. These were initially aimed at the air defence and air superiority roles. The most outstanding all-weather interceptor of the period was the McDonnell F-4 Phantom II, which in Vietnam was also used in the ground attack role. For fleet air defence the F-4 has largely been replaced by the Grumman F-14A Tomcat, with long-range AIM-54 Phoenix missiles, capable of killing at around 160 km (100 miles).

The Vietnam War stressed the need for air superiority at long range. This led to the massive McDonnell Douglas F-15 Eagle, the comparatively small General Dynamics F-16 Fighting Falcon, and the medium-size McDonnell Douglas F/A-18 Hornet naval fighter.

The ground attack field has seen a return to slower, heavily-armoured aircraft, such as the Fairchild A-10 and the Su-25 Frogfoot, which has been used against rebels in Afghanistan. The

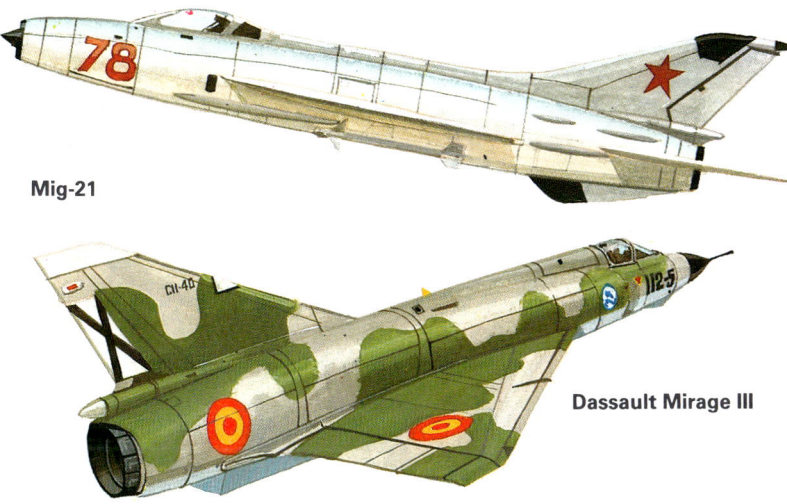

Mig-21

Dassault Mirage III

most remarkable advance is perhaps the British Aerospace Harrier family, with V/STOL (vertical or short take-off and landing) performance. Variable-sweep wings are used on several aircraft to win special advantages in airfield performance, patrol endurance or a smooth ride in high speed penetration.

Modern Airliners
The main advances in the commercial transport field have been linked with the use of new engine categories, new wing shapes and larger aircraft to improve economics. Aircraft such as the Vickers Viscount and Fokker F27 introduced turboprops – turbine engines driving propellers. The DH Comet, Boeing 707 and Sud Aviation Caravelle brought pure jet propulsion and various degrees of wing sweep. The Boeing 747 combined a wide-body cabin with highly economical turbofan engines, and the Airbus A300 brought these advantages to much shorter routes. The Anglo-French Concorde made possible Mach 2 cruise across the Atlantic, a fantastic technological achievement by any standard.

In less than 80 years aviation has progressed from the first tentative hops by the Wright Flyer to cruise at twice the speed of sound across an ocean, and vertical take-off and landing by high-speed combat aircraft. The following chapters discuss in more detail where military and civil aviation stand today, and how they are likely to develop in the future.

Military Aircraft Today

There are many different types of military aircraft. Most of them – apart from the smaller combat aircraft, such as fighters and ground attack aircraft – are similar to civil designs. So what are the differences?

Military Transports
A 'tactical' (short-to-medium range) military transport differs from its commercial counterpart largely in being designed to carry bulky loads such as armoured vehicles and to operate from short, makeshift airfields. Aircraft such as the C-130 Hercules and Transall have a very low floor and a rear loading ramp; rear-loading means that vehicles can be driven straight on. Sitting low on the ground, the aircraft has a short, strong undercarriage with low pressure tyres to suit unpaved surfaces. The wing is set high; ground clearance considerations rule out a low wing. Because it is primarily intended to transport rectangular loads, the fuselage tends to be squarer in shape than that of a commercial transport plane.

Patrolling the Sea
Maritime patrol aircraft are also closely related to commercial transports. The Fokker F27 Maritime is derived from the Friendship airliner, the Nimrod from the Comet, and the P-3C from the Electra. In order to convert a civilian transport plane into a maritime patrol a number of changes have to be made. These include fitting a sea-search radar, bulged observation windows and a new cabin interior. It may also mean putting in special navigation equipment, especially if the aircraft is to provide evidence of illegal fishing. Maritime search and rescue (SAR) aircraft may need provisions to drop flares, a dinghy, etc. If the aircraft is being adapted for anti-submarine warfare (ASW) it will need to be fitted with sonobuoys. Sonobuoys are special sensors which detect sound waves sent out from or reflected by submarines. Another piece of special equipment required in this role is the magnetic anomaly detection (MAD) 'sting'. This is a device which looks for changes

◀ **A demonstration of Embraer EMB-312 Tucano**
tandem-seat turboprop trainers. The Tucano was designed to imitate the engine handling of jet aircraft for military training.

in the Earth's magnetic field, indicating the presence of a large mass of metal. ASW aircraft carry lightweight torpedoes, either on external pylons or in an internal weapons bay. Maritime patrol aircraft are now being fitted with air-to-surface missiles so that they can engage ships from a safe distance.

Refuelling in the Sky

Flight refuelling tankers are usually conversions of existing transports, bombers or attack aircraft, such as the VC10, Tu-16 and KA-6D. In order to convert aircraft for this role, extra fuel tanks have to be installed. The aircraft also has to be fitted with special equipment to transfer fuel to another plane. The British services and the US Navy use a system known as 'probe-and-drogue'. The 'drogue' is a funnel attached to the end of a hose which is unreeled from the tanker. The 'probe' is a slender metal pipe attached to the front of the receiver aircraft. The pilot of the receiver aircraft flies his aircraft's probe into the drogue. This system, which leaves the pilot of the receiver aircraft to make contact, has the advantage that almost any type of aircraft can be made into a tanker. With a little additional plumbing, a combat aircraft can be used as a tanker to refuel similar aircraft – a system known as 'buddy-refuelling'. It can be converted back to its full operational role whenever necessary. The probe-and-drogue system also allows a large aircraft such as a Victor to refuel three fighters simultaneously, using one unit in the rear fuselage and one

▼ **The de Havilland Canada DHC-5 Buffalo**
transport aircraft in the markings of the
Canadian Armed Forces.

▲ **An A-4 Skyhawk** equipped with a hose and
drogue for in flight refuelling.

under either wing. Because the diameter of the hose restricts the
amount of fuel that can be transferred from one aircraft to
another, this system is best suited to refuelling small aircraft such
as fighters.

The United States Air Force has chosen another system of
refuelling, known as the 'flying boom' system. In this system the
tanker has a single refuelling unit in the rear fuselage. This consists
of a telescopic 'boom' or pipe. The boom is flown with the help of
two small wings. An operator inside the tanker is able to move the
boom by changing the angle of these wings. The 'receiver' aircraft
has a 'receptacle' (a refuelling point at the bottom of a funnel-
shaped slipway) in its upper fuselage. The pilot of the receiver flies
to a suitable position below the tanker, guided by the refuelling
operator in the tanker. The operator is able to 'fly' the boom so
that it makes contact with the receptacle. A tanker adapted to use
this system can transfer fuel at a far faster rate than one with a
hose and drogue. This makes it suitable for refuelling even the
heaviest bombers.

Radars and Radomes

Most airborne early warning (AEW) aircraft are also usually converted from transport aircraft. The Grumman E-2 Hawkeye is an exception. It was designed specifically for AEW duties although it is partly based on the C-2 Greyhound carrier onboard delivery (COD) aircraft. AEW aircraft have to be fitted with a massive antenna (or antennas) which gives an all-round field of view and enables targets to be detected at very long ranges. In most cases the radar uses two very long antennas which rotate inside a 'flying saucer' radome. In general the radome turns with the antennas, although the old Grumman E-1B Tracer has a fixed oval radome. The Nimrod AEW3 is unique in having two enormous radomes, one on the nose and one on the tail, instead of the normal flying saucer. This arrangement probably has less effect on the aircraft's performance and handling.

AEW aircraft have to be able to detect targets at very long range. They must also have facilities for transmitting the information to other aircraft, ships and military installations on the ground. AEW aircraft can also assist other aircraft in different ways; they can direct fighters and strike aircraft to their targets and back to base, or guide them around mountains or enemy defences.

THE SWING WING For high-speed flight the delta wing is ideal as it minimizes drag. But at take-off and during landing this design is less successful because it does not provide as much lift as the straight wing does. The variable sweep wing or 'swing wing' solves this problem. For take-off, landing and slow-speed flight the wing is moved forward into the straight wing shape. For high speed the wings are pivoted back to give a swept wing or delta shape.

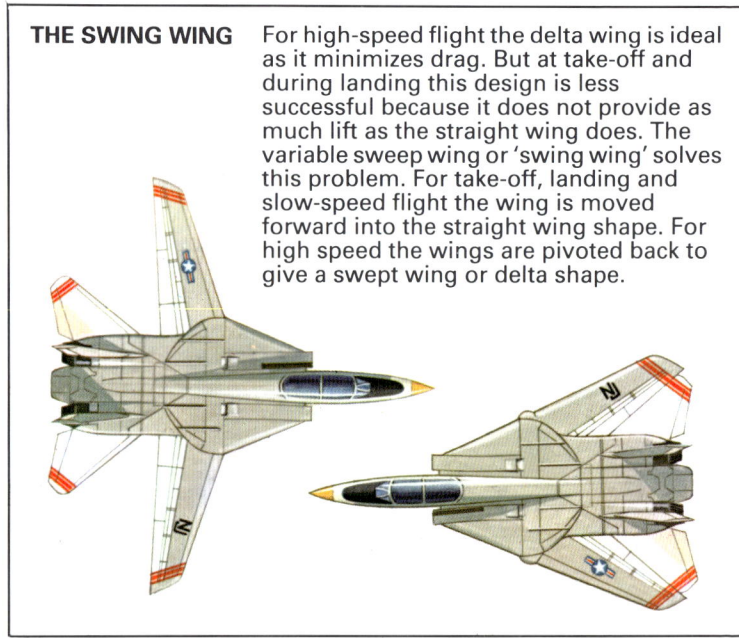

▲ **The Boeing E-3A Sentry** is often referred to simply as AWACS (Airborne Warning and Control System).

Electronic Warfare

The main purpose of the electronic warfare (EW) aircraft is to jam enemy radars, in order to deny them information on the position of friendly aircraft.

Some EW aircraft are adaptations of transport aircraft. The Ilyushin Il-20, for example, is derived from the I1-18 airliner. Where this is the case, the aircraft is limited to operations outside the reach of enemy defences. If the EW aircraft is to penetrate with the strike aircraft, it is usually a derivative of the aircraft carrying the bombs. The Grumman EF-111A and EA-6B are examples of this type of conversion. Equipment has to be installed to receive and record enemy radar transmissions, and to transmit signals that will jam the enemy receivers, reducing the information they would otherwise obtain. A very powerful transmitter, that can transmit on several frequency bands, is needed to jam a ground-based radar successfully. This is why EW aircraft have so many antennas and jammer pods.

Special avionics installations are also used on airborne command post aircraft to permit secure communications with a variety of military units in the air, at sea and on ground. Many transport aircraft have been converted to this role, from the C-47 to the Boeing 747 (redesignated E-4B).

▲ **The SR-71A Blackbird** is the ultimate reconnaissance aircraft. It holds the world record for sustained height and for speed.

Reconnaissance and Observation

Reconnaissance and observation aircraft tend to be designed specifically for these roles, although it is possible to convert other aircraft for short-range reconnaissance. A Jaguar or a Tornado can be fitted with a special camera pod and an RF-4C Phantom II is equipped with a nose full of sensors. But long-range penetration calls for a 'dedicated' reconnaissance plane.

In the past, aircraft have been selected for this role because they have been able to fly above the enemy's defences. A classic example of this was the Lockheed U-2 which could fly well above Soviet fighters. But after a U-2 piloted by Gary Powers was shot down near Sverdlovsk on 1 May 1960, flights over the Soviet Union ceased. Another approach is to use aircraft that can see deep into enemy territory, while flying just outside its national limits. The latest member of the U-2 family is the TR-1A which uses a side-looking airborne radar (SLAR) and can see approximately 55 kilometres (35 miles) into enemy territory.

Lockheed are also responsible for the legendary SR-71A Blackbird. The U-2 had been designed to achieve long-range at high altitude. The SR-71 combines these features with extremely high speed (approximately Mach 3). Aerodynamic efficiency at a high Mach number is obtained by use of a slender delta wing. Special heat-resistant materials are used to withstand the high temperatures encountered during high-altitude, high-speed cruising.

Tactical observation aircraft such as the Grumman OV-1 and Rockwell OV-10 are traditionally used to direct artillery fire and strikes by supporting aircraft. They have to be capable of short take-off and landing (STOL) so that they can operate close to the front line. Visibility from the cockpit is also an important design factor. These planes are usually armed for self-defence and target marking (using smoke rockets). They need to be able to fly slowly to detect concealed targets but this makes them vulnerable to return fire. These aircraft would probably not be used in a full-scale war but they are still useful in counter-insurgency (COIN) situations.

◀ **The Aérospatiale** AS **355 M Ecureuil 2/ TwinStar** six-seat light general-purpose utility helicopter.

Military Helicopters

Military helicopters are usually very similar to civilian models although they are far less comfortable inside. They are also equipped to carry armament and they need some protection against bullet strikes. The army attack helicopter is a special case as it has to engage armour in the area of battle. The very slender fuselage is designed to make the aircraft less vulnerable from the front. The army attack helicopter carries anti-tank guided weapons.

Experts disagree over the best place to position the sight head. A mast mounted sight (MMS) above the rotor allows the helicopter to fire from behind cover, but it is difficult to engineer. A roof-mounted sight is favoured in Europe. This system puts

43

most of the helicopter behind cover, although the rotor is still exposed. Doppler radars, which respond to target movement, would detect the rotor very easily. A chin-mounted sight, favoured by the United States, exposes the whole helicopter but allows very sophisticated and heavy sensors to be used.

Another special case is the ASW helicopter, which must carry sonobuoys or dipping sonar to detect the submarine, radar to spot a periscope or 'snorkel', and lightweight torpedoes to attack the submarine. Naval helicopters are also used in a variety of tasks, including mine countermeasures using towed 'sweeps'.

▼ **The MBB BO 105 P (PAH-1)** equipped with Hot anti-tank missiles.

Fixed-Wing Trainers

There are three main categories of fixed-wing trainer: primary, basic and advanced. The primary trainer is usually a cheap piston-engined aircraft, to test the student's general aptitude. A number of students are eliminated at this early stage. Some suffer incurably from airsickness. Others find it impossible to judge heights accurately and this makes them incapable of landing aircraft safely. Because military standards are much higher than civilian ones, the primary trainer is far more powerful and difficult to fly than a club aircraft. The military trainer is normally fully aerobatic, whereas many civil trainers are only semi-aerobatic.

The student may spend 20–30 hours on the primary trainer, with some time flying solo. He will then progress to the basic trainer and may easily spend 100–150 hours on this second stage. Until recently, turbojet aircraft – such as the Aermacchi MB.326 and the

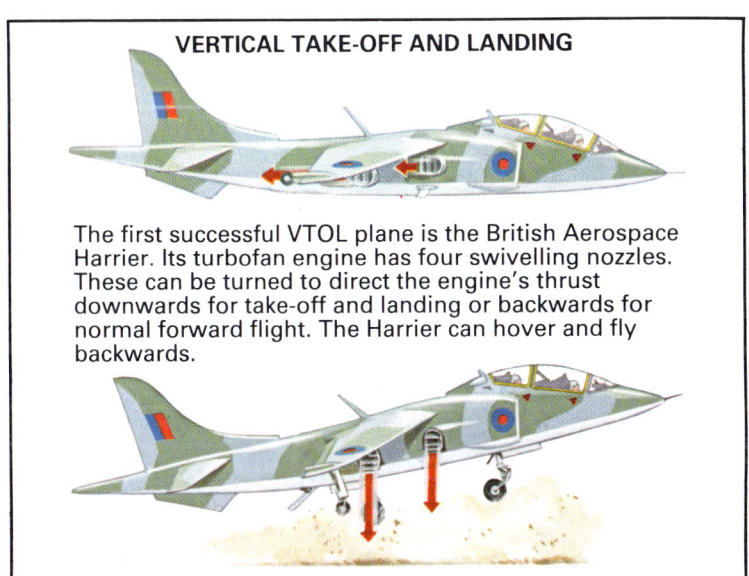

VERTICAL TAKE-OFF AND LANDING

The first successful VTOL plane is the British Aerospace Harrier. Its turbofan engine has four swivelling nozzles. These can be turned to direct the engine's thrust downwards for take-off and landing or backwards for normal forward flight. The Harrier can hover and fly backwards.

Cessna T-37 – were used for basic training. The need to cut costs now favours turboprop or turbofan aircraft, which burn less fuel.

At the end of the basic training stage, some air forces save money by dividing the students according to whether they have been selected to fly the fast jets, large multi-engined aircraft or helicopters. Other services take all the students through advanced jet training, despite the high costs involved.

The advanced jet trainer is flown for 80–120 hours. The student may then have a further 50 hours of preliminary tactical (or weapon) training on a different aircraft. Some air forces give tactical training on the aircraft that the student is to fly operationally. Until recently people were very keen on the idea of a supersonic advanced trainer, such as the Northrop T-38. But such aircraft are very expensive to operate because of their afterburning engines. It is now felt that the extra cost is not justified by the training value of a short burst of supersonic speed. It is more important to train the student in low-level navigation exercises at speeds in the region of Mach 0.7.

Combat Aircraft – Shaped for Speed
Most military aircraft are, as we have seen, related to civil designs, but combat aircraft are completely different from any civil types. Whereas civil aircraft are designed mainly to cruise economically,

combat aircraft are designed for brief dashes at high speed, a high rate of climb and a good combat ceiling.

Ground attack aircraft can generally reach around Mach 0·9 at sea level in a clean condition (without external stores). Some strike aircraft can attain Mach 1·1–1·2 at sea level, though such speeds would only be used for a short penetration or escape. The fastest fighters can also reach such speeds at low level, but they can fly much faster in the thinner air at higher levels. The F-15 can probably touch Mach 2·5 at around 11,000 metres (36,000 feet). Above Mach 2·5 aerodynamic heating is a serious problem for aluminium structures, and so time in this region has to be limited.

▼ **The Northrop F-20 Tigershark**

Supersonic speed demands low wave drag, which means a slender fuselage and a thin, swept wing. The delta wing (e.g. Mirage III) provides an excellent combination of low wave drag and large fuel volume. However, until recently the delta has tended to penalize both turning and airfield performance. A better compromise was achieved with a moderately swept wing (e.g. Mirage F.1). Variable-sweep wings (or 'swing-wings') such as those of the F-14, F-111 and Tornado improve airfield performance, loiter performance, and gust response in low-level penetration, but they make the aircraft very heavy.

Two of the most important developments of recent years have been artificial stability and electrically-signalled flying controls ('fly-by-wire'). A conventional aircraft has its centre of gravity well forward for stability, and wing lift is trimmed by a download on the tailplane. In a turn, the wing lift is increased, and so is the trimming download, which reduces turning performance. If artificial ('black box') stability is used, sending electrical signals to

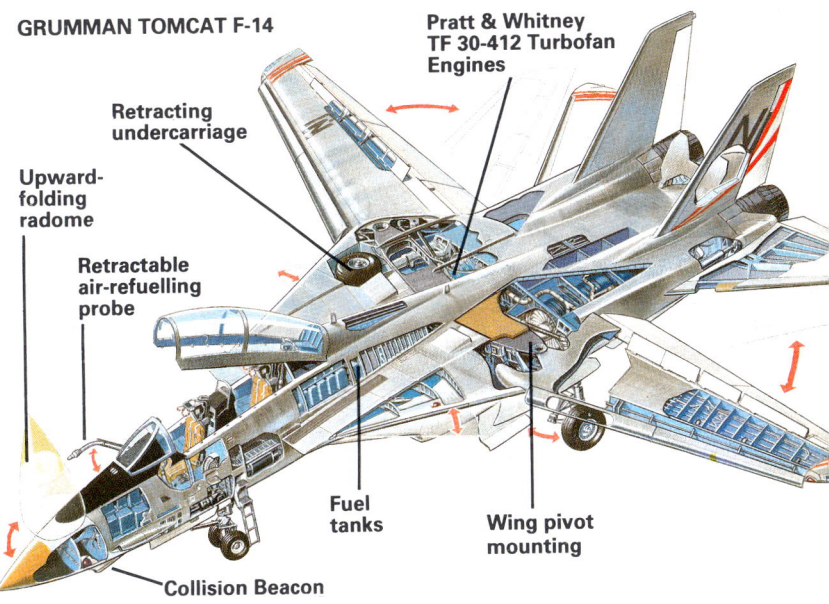

GRUMMAN TOMCAT F-14

Pratt & Whitney TF 30-412 Turbofan Engines

Retracting undercarriage

Upward-folding radome

Retractable air-refuelling probe

Fuel tanks

Wing pivot mounting

Collision Beacon

the tailplane, the centre of gravity can be moved farther aft, allowing the tail to carry an upload. This system benefits conventional aircraft such as the F-16, but it is of even greater benefit in the case of a delta wing.

Innovation and Design

One of the fundamental decisions in designing a fighter is how many engines to use. A single-engined aircraft is generally simpler and cheaper than a twin. A twin, on the other hand, should provide a lower accident rate (since it may be able to return to base after one engine fails) and probably fewer losses in battle. In practice, the decision is often dictated by engine availability. Small fighters tend to be single-engined (the Northrop F-5 is a notable exception), and large fighters (such as F-15) have to be twins because there are no correspondingly powerful engines. Air intakes tend to be placed underneath a flat surface (see F-16 and F/A-18), because this will direct air straight at the inlet, even when the fighter is nose-high in a turn. In the case of an aircraft designed using 'stealth' (or 'low observable') technology, the inlets may be placed in the aircraft's upper surface to minimize their exposure to ground radars. The full use of stealth technology results in a shape very different from the normal combat aircraft, and this approach

▲ **The Dassault-Breguet Mirage 2000B** armed with bombs, air-to-air missiles and drop tanks.

is probably only justified for deep penetrations of enemy territory. Most combat aircraft will rely on radar-absorbent materials in the air intakes, and special camouflage schemes to reduce detection probability.

The main trend in fighter design is to canard (tail-first) layouts with a wing shape that is a combination of delta and swept wing. This will combine the volume and wave drag advantages of the delta with the better low-speed turning performance of the swept wing. The forward-swept wing, made possible by advanced composite materials, is also being tested, and may provide improved manoeuvrability. Another important change will be the use of 'two-dimensional' (i.e. rectangular) jetpipe nozzles. These will make it far easier to reverse thrust to shorten the landing run.

A major advance in fighter equipment is provided by Doppler radars, which can detect low-flying aircraft. Modern radars have track-while-scan capability, which means they can track the main target while searching for others. A lot of effort is going into developing radars that can actually identify the target, allowing it to be attacked from beyond visual range (BVR).

In the field of air-to-air guided weapons, some missiles now have radars as effective as those in earlier fighters. The development of miniature computers is making possible multi-stage guidance systems allowing firing at much longer ranges. For example, a missile may start out on autopilot toward a predicted target

▲ The General Dynamics F-16A Fighting Falcon in
the fighter/bomber role.

position, then receive a target update from the fighter radar, and
only as a third stage switch on its own sensor. Infra-red homing
missiles, which at present are easily decoyed by flares or by the Sun,
will soon be able to examine the shape of the target and calculate its
speed. Helmet-mounted sights (HMS) will allow the fighter pilot to
fire missiles at targets at large angles from his line of flight.

Important armament developments are also taking place in the
field of ground attack. The main objective is to be able to deliver
weapons without flying directly over the target. This may mean
giving the weapon flip-out wings, a guidance system, and some
form of powerplant.

At the lower end of the scale, close support aircraft (ground
attack aircraft giving direct support to friendly troops) will have to
fly faster, to avoid being shot down by man-portable surface-to-air
missiles (SAMs). But higher speeds will make it more difficult for
them to identify their targets. In the longer term, their role may be
increasingly taken over by artillery.

At the opposite extreme, the major question as far as long-range
strike aircraft and bombers are concerned is whether deep
penetrations of enemy territory will remain feasible. It remains to
be seen whether tomorrow's penetrator should stay low and rely
on jamming the AEW radar, or fly high and rely on stealth
technology. Alternatively, the tasks of strike and reconnaissance
may best be taken over by remotely launched missiles.

49

AIR FORCE INSIGNIAS

1 Afghanistan; 2 Albania; 3 Algeria; 4 Argentina; 5 Argentina (Navy); 6 Australia; 7 Austria; 8 Bangladesh; 9 Barbados; 10 Belgium; 11 Benin; 12 Bolivia; 13 Brazil; 14 Brazil (Navy); 15 Brunei; 16 Bulgaria; 17 Burma; 18 Cameroon; 19 Canada; 20 Central African Republic; 21 Chad; 22 Chile; 23 China (People's Republic); 24 China (Nationalist Republic); 25 Colombia; 26 Congo; 27 Cuba; 28 Czechoslovakia; 29 Denmark; 30 Dominica; 31 Ecuador; 32 Egypt;

33 Ethiopia; 34 Finland; 35 France; 36 France (Navy);
37 Gabon; 38 Germany (Democratic Republic); 39 Germany
(Federal Republic); 40 Ghana; 41 Greece; 42 Guatemala;
43 Guinea; 44 Guyana; 45 Haiti; 46 Honduras; 47 Hungary;
48 India; 49 Indonesia; 50 Indonesia (Navy);
51 Indonesia (Army); 52 Iran; 53 Iraq; 54 Ireland; 55 Israel;
56 Italy; 57 Ivory Coast; 58 Jamaica; 59 Japan; 60 Jordan;
61 Kenya; 62 Korea (North); 63 Korea (South); 64 Kuwait;

AIR FORCE INSIGNIAS

65 Lebanon; 66 Libya; 67 Madagascar; 68 Malawi;
69 Malaysia; 70 Mali; 71 Mauretania; 72 Mexico;
73 Mongolia; 74 Morocco; 75 Nepal; 76 Netherlands;
77 New Zealand; 78 Nicaragua; 79 Niger; 80 Nigeria;
81 Norway; 82 Oman; 83 Pakistan; 84 Panama; 85 Papua
New Guinea; 86 Paraguay; 87 Peru; 88 Peru (Navy);
89 Philippines; 90 Poland; 91 Portugal; 92 Qatar;
93 Zimbabwe; 94 Romania; 95 Rwanda; 96 Salvador;

97   Saudi Arabia;   98   Senegal;   99   Singapore;   100   Somalia;
101   South Africa;   102 Soviet Union;   103   Spain;   104 Sri Lanka;
105   Sudan;   106   Sweden;   107   Switzerland;   108   Syria;
109   Tanzania;   110   Thailand;   111   Togo;   112   Trinidad and Tobago;
113   Tunisia;   114   Turkey;   115   Uganda;   116   United Arab Emirates;
117   United Kingdom;   118 United Kingdom (camouflaged);   119   United
States;   120   Upper Volta;   121   Uruguay;   122   Venezuela;
123   Vietnam;   125   Yemen (Arab Republic);   124   Yemen (People's
Democratic Republic);   126   Yugoslavia;   127   Zaire;   128   Zambia.

Fighters

Mirage III

The Dassault-Breguet Mirage III is Europe's most successful post-war fighter series. The first prototype flew on 17 November 1956, and almost 1500 have now been built. Note the simple delta wing shape and half-cone intakes.

Wing span: 8·22 m (26 ft. 11½ in.)
Length: 15·03 m (49 ft. 3½ in.)
Max speed: Mach 2·2 or 2330 km/h (1455 mph)

Mirage F.1

The Dassault-Breguet Mirage F.1 largely superseded the III/5 series. Instead of the pure delta the F.1 has a swept wing. This gives shorter airfield demands and makes it more suitable for ground attack. Over 700 have now been ordered.

Wing span: 8·4 m (27 ft. 6½ in.)
Length: 15.30 m (50 ft. 2½ in.)
Max speed: Mach 2·2 or 2330 km/h (1455 mph)

Mirage 2000

The Dassault-Breguet Mirage 2000 represents a return by this French manufacturer to the delta formula. Technically, it is very different from the III/5 series. Externally, it is more refined, with the wing blended into the fuselage, and a fin like that of the F.1.

Wing span: 9·0 m (29 ft. 6 in.)
Length: 14·50 m (47 ft. 7 in.)
Max speed: over Mach 2·3 or 2440 km/h (1520 mph)

Super Etcndard

The Dassault-Breguet Super Etendard is an updated version of the earlier Etendard IV-M. It has a more powerful engine and new avionics, including a nose radar. A carrier-based fighter, it can be used for both air defence and anti-shipping strike duties.

Wing span: 9·6 m (31 ft. 6in.)
Length: 14·31 m (46 ft. 11½ in.)
Max speed: approx Mach 1 or 1060 km/h (661 mph)

Tornado F.2

The Panavia Tornado ADV (air defence variant) is an interceptor version of the original strike fighter, developed for Britain's RAF. Designated the Tornado F Mk 2, it is slightly longer than the earlier model, has a more slender nose and is painted pale grey.

Wing span: 13·9 m (45 ft. 7 in.) to 8·6 m (28 ft. 2½ in.)
Length: 18·06 m (59 ft. 3 in.)
Max speed: Mach 2·2 or 2330 km/h (1455 mph)

Kfir

The Israel Aircraft Industries Kfir (Lion Cub) is derived from the Mirage 5, but has a far more powerful engine (the GE J79, like that in the Phantom) and many other improvements. It can be recognized by changes to the rear fuselage and nose shape. The latest model has canards on the intakes.

Wing span: 8·22 m (26 ft. 11½ in.)
Length: 15·65 m (51 ft. 4½ in.)
Max speed: Mach 2·3 or 2440 km/h (1520 mph)

Draken

The Saab-Scania Draken has a unique double-delta or compound-delta wing, which gives more stowage volume than the simple delta of the Mirage III/5. Over 600 were produced for service in Denmark, Finland and Sweden.

Wing span: 9·42 m (30 ft. 10½ in.)
Length: 14·28 m (46 ft. 10½ in.)
Max speed: Mach 2 or 2120 km/h (1320 mph)

JA37 Viggen

The Saab-Scania JA37 Viggen (Thunderbolt) is an air defence version of the earlier strike/reconnaissance aircraft. It has a more powerful engine and new avionics. The JA37 can be recognized by its cranked fin-tip and belly-mounted cannon. Note the canards and double-delta wing.

Wing span: 10·6 m (34 ft. 8½ in.)
Length: 16·4 m (53 ft. 9½ in.)
Max speed: over Mach 2 or 2120 km/h (1320 mph)

MiG-21 Fishbed

The Mikoyan MiG-21 (NATO code-name Fishbed) first flew on 16 June 1956, and the type is now one of the most widely used fighters. Over 10,000 have been built for service in more than 30 countries. The combination of delta wing and conventional tail is distinctive.

Wing span: 7·15 m (23 ft. 5½ in.)
Length: 15·76 m (51 ft. 8½ in.)
Max speed: Mach 2·1 or 2225 km/h (1385 mph)

57

MiG-23 Flogger

The Mikoyan MiG-23 (NATO code-name Flogger) was first shown in public in 1967, and was one of the Soviet Union's first swing-wing fighters. Note the high-set wing with massive leading-edge extensions, and the shape of the fin. The nose radar distinguishes it from the MiG-27, which is also code-named Flogger.

Wing span: approx 14·25 (46 ft. 9 in.) to 8·17 m (26 ft. 9½ in.)
Length: approx 16·8 m (55 ft. 1½ in.)
Max speed: approx Mach 2·3 or 2440 km/h (1520 mph)

MiG-25 Foxbat

The Mikoyan MiG-25 (NATO code-name Foxbat) is one of the fastest production aircraft in the world, rivalling the Lockheed SR-71A. The SR-71A holds the world speed record, but the MiG-25 holds the altitude record with a zoom to 37,650 m (123,523 ft.) in 1977. The MiG-25 exists in both interceptor and reconnaissance forms.

Wing span: 13·95 m (45 ft. 9 in.)
Length: 23·82 m (44 ft. 0 in.)
Max speed: approx Mach 2·8 or 2970 km/h (1850 mph)

Su-15 Flagon

The Sukhoi Su-15 (NATO code-name Flagon) is a twin-engined interceptor, rather like a big MiG-21, but with side intakes to allow a large nose radar, and with cranked leading edges to its delta wing. It was an Su-15 that shot down the Korean Air Lines Boeing 747 off Sakhalin on 1 September 1983.

Wing span: approx 10·5 m (34 ft. 5 in.)
Length: approx 20·5 m (68 ft. 0 in.)
Max speed: approx Mach 2·3 or 2440 km/h (1520 mph)

Tu-28P Fiddler

The Tupolev Tu-28P/Tu-128 (NATO code-name Fiddler) is the largest fighter in the world. Powered by two afterburning engines, it is probably used to defend areas where radars and airfields are few and far between. Note the wing undercarriage fairings, a feature of many Tupolev designs.

Wing span: approx 20 m (65 ft. 7 in.)
Length: approx 26 m (85 ft. 3 in.)
Max speed: approx Mach 1·6 or 1695 km/h (1060 mph)

Yak-28P Firebar

The Yakovlev Yak-28P (NATO code-name Firebar) is a two-seat all-weather interceptor, powered by two of the engines used in the MiG-21. Some Firebars have a remarkably long nose radome. The nose radar distinguishes Firebar from the Yak-28 Brewer light bomber and reconnaissance aircraft, which has a glazed nose occupied by a navigator/bomb-aimer.

Wing span: approx 13 m (42 ft. 7½ in.)
Length: approx 21·5 m (70 ft. 6 in.)
Max speed: approx Mach 1·50 or 1590 km/h (990 mph)

Sea Harrier

The British Aerospace Sea Harrier FRS Mk 1 achieved great distinction in the Falklands conflict of 1982, destroying 23 Argentine aircraft without a single loss in air combat. The Sea Harrier is flown by the Royal Navy and Indian Navy. It differs from the RAF Harrier in having a radar nose and raised cockpit.

Wing span: 7·7 m (25 ft. 3 in.)
Length: 14·5 m (47 ft. 7 in.)
Max speed: 1175 km/h (735 mph)

Lightning

The British Aerospace Lightning was (in its day) one of the fastest-climbing interceptors in the world. It has served with both the RAF and Royal Saudi Air Force. The highly swept wing, deep fuselage and nose intake are easily recognized.

Wing span: 10·62 m (34 ft. 10 in.)
Length: 16·84 m (55 ft. 3 in.)
Max speed: over Mach 2·0 or 2120 km/h (1320 mph)

Fighting Falcon

F-16 Fighting Falcon

The General Dynamics F-16 Fighting Falcon is probably the finest dogfight aircraft in the world. Manoeuvrability benefits from its very high power, artificial stability, and wing-body blending. The pilot has a semi-reclined seat and a sidestick (a miniature control stick placed on a shelf beside the pilot).

Wing span: 9·45 m (31 ft. 0 in.)
Length: 15·09 m (49 ft. 6 in.)
Max speed: over Mach 2·0 or 2120 km/h (1320 mph)

F-14 Tomcat

The Grumman F-14 Tomcat was developed to replace the Phantom as a fleet air defence fighter for the US Navy. It also serves with the Iranian Air Force. This swing-wing twin-engined fighter can fire Phoenix missiles with a range of up to 160 km (100 miles). Note the twin fins, the intake design, and widely spaced engines.

Wing span: 19·54 m (64 ft. 1½ in.) to 11·65 m (38 ft. 2½ in.)
Length: 19·1 m (62 ft. 8 in.)
Max speed: Mach 2·34 or 2480 km/h (1545 mph)

F-104 Starfighter

The Lockheed F-104G Starfighter is a multi-role fighter, developed primarily for the low-level nuclear strike role in Europe. It is unusual in having a straight wing, although its aerofoil section is remarkably thin. Note the high-set tail.

Wing span: 6·68 m (21 ft. 11 in.)
Length: 16·69 m (54 ft. 9 in.)
Max speed: Mach 2·34 or 2480 km/h (1545 mph)

F-4 Phantom

The McDonnell Douglas F-4 Phantom II began life as a US Navy fleet air defence fighter. In the Vietnam War it was adapted to both the air superiority and ground attack roles. One of the most outstanding post-war fighters, it is identified by its sawn-off rear fuselage and sharply tapered wing with upturned tips.

Wing span: 11·7 m (38 ft. 4½ in.)
Length: 17·77 m (58 ft. 3½ in.)
Max speed: Mach 2·40 or 2540 km/h (1585 mph)

F-15 Eagle

The McDonnell Douglas F-15 Eagle is probably the world's finest all-weather air defence and air superiority fighter. Future development emphasizes the ground attack role. The F-15 has twin fins and a distinctive wing shape.

Wing span: 13·05 m (42 ft. 9½ in.)
Length: 19·43 m (63 ft. 9 in.)
Max speed: Mach 2·5 or 2650 km/h (1650 mph)

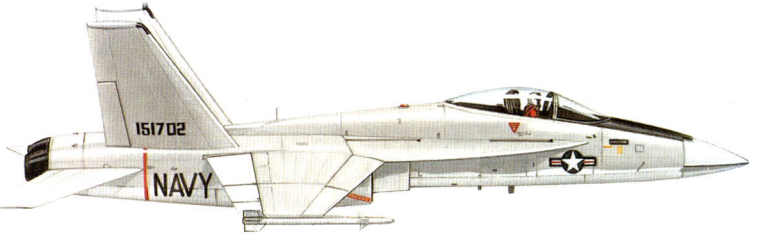

F/A-18 Hornet

The McDonnell Douglas F/A-18 Hornet is a fighter and attack aircraft, designed primarily as a complement for the F-14 and replacement for the A-7 in US Navy service. It is also being sold in Australia, Canada and Spain, for ground-based duties.

Wing span: 11·43 m (37 ft. 6 in.)
Length: 17·07 m (56 ft. 0 in.)
Max speed: Mach 1·8 or 1910 km/h (1190 mph)

F-5E Tiger II

The Northrop F-5E Tiger II is the second of the F-5 mini-fighter series, replacing the F-5A. While limited in its load-carrying capability and radius of action by its small size, the F-5E is a useful short-range dogfight aircraft. It is used by USAF 'Aggressor' training units.

Wing span: 8·13 m (26 ft. 8 in.)
Length: 14·17 m (46 ft. 6 in.)
Max speed: Mach 2 or 2120 km/h (1320 mph)

Wing span: 8·13 m (26 ft. 8 in.)
Length: 14·45 m (47 ft. 4¾ in.)
Max speed: Mach 1·64 or 1735 km/h (1085 mph)

F-20 Tigershark

The Northrop F-20 Tigershark is derived from the F-5 series, but has a large single engine (as used in the F/A-18) in place of the two small engines of the F-5E. The F-20 also introduces an advanced radar.

Ground Attack Aircraft and Bombers

IA-58 Pucará

The FMA (Fábrica Militar de Aviones) IA-58 Pucará is a twin-turboprop counter-insurgency aircraft, developed in Argentina. Although slow by jet standards, it performed quite well in the Falklands conflict, operating from grass airfields and roads.

Wing span: 14·5 m (47 ft. 6¾ in.)
Length: 14·25 m (46 ft. 9 in.)
Max speed: 500 km/h (310 mph)

Q-5 Fantan-A

The Nanchang Qiangjiji-5 (NATO code-name Fantan-A) is a Chinese derivative of the Soviet MiG-19 for ground attack duties. The Q-5 differs in having side intakes and a bomb-bay, although this bay is now used to house extra fuel tanks. Note the highly swept wing and large fences.

Wing span: 9·7 m (31 ft. 10 in.)
Length: 16·73 m (54 ft. 10½ in.)
Max speed: 1185 km/h (740 mph)

Mirage 5/50

The Dassault-Breguet Mirage 5/50 is a simply equipped ground attack version of the Mirage III, with a limited air defence capability. The Mirage 5 is distinguished by its very small nose ranging radar. The Mirage 50 has the more powerful engine of the Mirage F.1, and a larger nose radar, though in a more slender radome than for the Mirage III.

Wing span: 8·22 m (26 ft. 11½ in.)
Length: 15·55 m (51 ft. ½ in.)
Max speed: Mach 2·2 or 2330 km/h (1455 mph)

Mirage IVA

The Dassault-Breguet Mirage IVA, operating in conjunction with Boeing KC-135F tankers, is the basis of the French Air Force nuclear strike force. Looking rather like a large, twin-engined Mirage III, the IVA is unmistakable.

Wing span: 11·85 m (38 ft. 10¼ in.)
Length: 23·46 m (76 ft. 11¼ in.)
Max speed: Mach 2·2 or 2330 km/h (1455 mph)

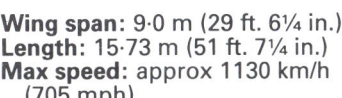

HF-24 Marut

The Hindustan Aeronautics Ltd HF-24 Marut (Wind Spirit) was the first combat aircraft of Indian design to reach production status. Powered by two afterburning versions of the engine used in the Gnat, the HF-24 was intended to be a multi-role aircraft, but was soon relegated to ground attack.

Wing span: 9·0 m (29 ft. 6¼ in.)
Length: 15·73 m (51 ft. 7¼ in.)
Max speed: approx 1130 km/h (705 mph)

AMX

The Aeritalia/Aermacchi/Embraer AMX is a ground attack aircraft jointly developed by Italy and Brazil. Using the same engine as the Vought A-7D/E in a smaller airframe, it will provide better airfield performance.

Wing span: 8·87 m (29 ft. 1½ in.)
Length: 13·58 m (44 ft. 6½ in.)
Max speed: approx 1120 km/h (700 mph)

Alpha Jet

The Dassault-Breguet/Dornier Alpha Jet was designed to be equally effective in the close support and pilot training roles. The German Air Force uses it both for ground attack and as an anti-helicopter aircraft. The German version has a pointed nose, but export dual-role versions have the rounded nose of the French trainer.

Wing span: 9·11 m (29 ft. 10¾ in.)
Length: 13·23 m (43 ft. 5 in.)
Max speed: 1040 km/h (645 mph)

Tornado IDS

Tornado IDS

The Panavia Tornado IDS (interdiction/strike) aircraft is a joint development by Britain, Italy and West Germany aimed mainly at the low level nuclear strike role. Its variable-sweep wing gives short take-off-and-landing distances, and reduced gust response.

Wing span: 13·9 m (45 ft. 7 in.) to 8·6 m (28 ft. 2½ in.)
Length: 16·7 m (54 ft. 9½ in.)
Max speed: Mach 2·2 or 2330 km/h (1455 mph)

Jaguar

The Sepecat Jaguar was jointly developed by Britain and France. It has two engines, afterburning versions of that used in the BAe Hawk. The Jaguar has been exported to Ecuador, India and Oman. The high wing and intakes, and the sawn-off rear fuselage are distinctive.

Wing span: 8·69 m (28 ft. 6 in.)
Length: 6·83 m (55 ft. 2½ in.)
Max speed: Mach 1·6 or 1695 km/h (1060 mph)

IAR-93 Orao

The SOKO/CNIAR IAR-93 Orao (Eagle) is a joint development by Romania and Yugoslavia, aimed at close support and ground attack duties. Powered by two engines of the type used in the Aermacchi MB-339, the later IAR-93B has afterburners. The aircraft is generally similar in appearance to the Jaguar, but without the sawn-off jetpipes.

Wing span: 9·62 m (31 ft. 6¾ in.)
Length: 14·9 m (48 ft. 10½ in.)
Max speed: 1160 km/h (720 mph)

AJ37 Viggen

The Saab-Scania AJ37 Viggen is a multi-role combat aircraft with emphasis on ground attack duties. Unconventional in design, it pioneered the use of a canard layout for short field performance, allowing it to operate in wartime from dispersed sites on Sweden's highways.

Wing span: 10·6 m (34 ft. 8½ in.)
Length: 16·4 m (53 ft. 9½in.)
Max speed: approx Mach 1·7 or 1800 km/h (1055 mph)

MiG-27 Flogger

The Mikoyan MiG-27 (NATO code-name Flogger) is a ground attack version of the MiG-23, with much simpler avionics and fixed intakes. The MiG-27 has a sharply tapered nose, which appears to house a small radar.

Wing span: approx 14·25 m (46 ft. 9 in.) to 8·17 m (26 ft. 9½ in.)
Length: approx 16·0 m (52 ft. 6 in.)
Max speed: approx Mach 1·7 or 1800 km/h (1055 mph)

Su-17 Fitter

Su-17/20/22 Fitter

The Sukhoi Su-17 series is a swing-wing family of ground attack aircraft, derived from the earlier fixed-wing Su-7 (also code-named Fitter). The Su-20 is a simply equipped export version. The Su-22 is believed to be an export aircraft with the more powerful engine used in the MiG-27.

Wing span: approx 14·0 m (45 ft. 11¼ in.) to 10·6 m (34 ft. 9½ in.)
Length: approx 18·75 m (50 ft. 6¼ in.)
Max speed: approx Mach 2·0 or 2120 km/h (1320 mph)

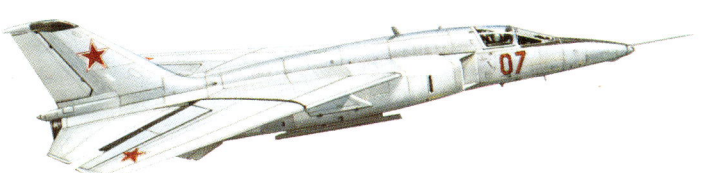

Su-24 Fencer

The Sukhoi Su-24 (NATO code-name Fencer) is a swing-wing strike fighter in broadly the same class as America's F-111A. It may also have an air-to-air role, threatening air reinforcements across the North Atlantic. Note the bulky fuselage, sharply tapered nose and slender wings.

Wing span: approx 17·0 m (55 ft. 9 in.) to 10·5 m (34 ft. 5 in.)
Length: approx 18·75 m (61 ft. 6 in.)
Max speed: approx Mach 2·0 or 2120 km/h (1320 mph)

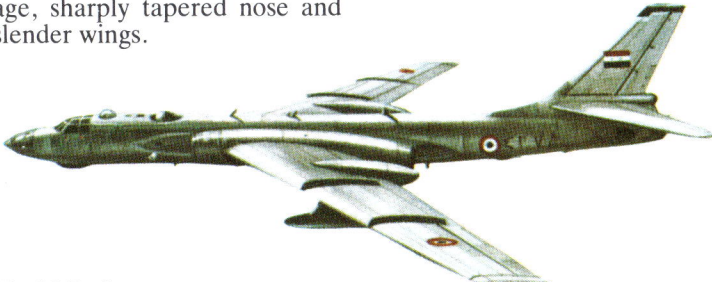

Tu-16 Badger

The Tupolev Tu-16 (NATO code-name Badger) is an old Soviet bomber, which first flew in 1952. It was probably intended for strikes against Western Europe, but it is now used as a tanker and as a reconnaissance and electronics warfare aircraft. Soviet Naval Aviation also uses it to provide an anti-shipping strike capability with large air-to-surface missiles.

Wing span: 32·93 m (108 ft. 0 in.)
Length: 34·8 m (114 ft. 2 in.)
Max speed: approx 900 km/h (565 mph)

Tu-95 Bear

The Tupolev Tu-95 (NATO code-name Bear) is almost as old as the Tu-16, having first flown in 1954. Incredibly, the Tu-95 is still in production as a parent aircraft for long-range cruise missiles. The type is also used for maritime patrol and anti-submarine warfare (ASW). The Tu-95 can be distinguished from the Tu-114 commercial transport by the latter's much fatter fuselage.

Wing span: approx 51 m (167 ft. 3 in.)
Length: approx 49·5 m (162 ft. 4 in.)
Max speed: approx 900 km/h (565 mph)

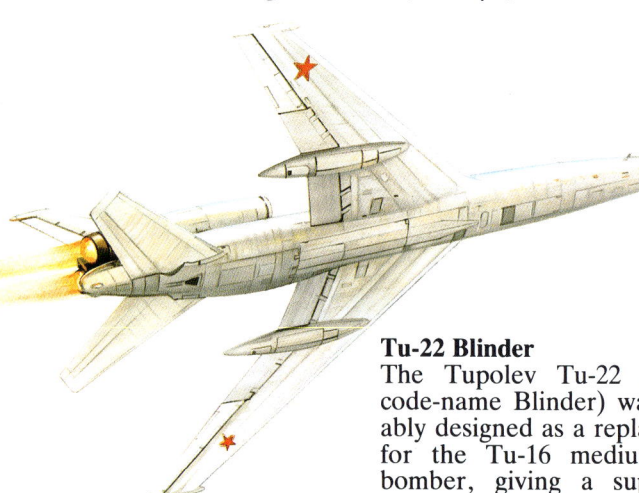

Tu-22 Blinder

The Tupolev Tu-22 (NATO code-name Blinder) was probably designed as a replacement for the Tu-16 medium-range bomber, giving a supersonic dash capability. It is thought that about 250 were built for strike and reconnaissance duties. The engine location is unique. Note the main undercarriage fairings on the wing.

Wing span: approx 27·5m (90 ft 2½ in.)
Length: approx 40·5 m (132 ft. 10 in.)
Max speed: approx Mach 1·5 or 1590 km/h (990 mph)

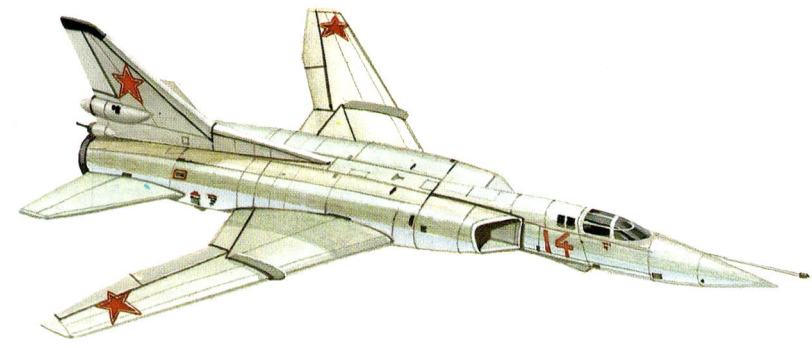

Tu-22M Backfire

The Tupolev Tu-22M (NATO code-name Backfire) is the most modern Soviet Bomber in service, although the even more advanced Blackjack is being developed. Over 250 Backfires have been built, and production continues at around 30 units each year. It is capable of long-range strike, anti-ship, and reconnaissance missions. Backfire is often seen with external bomb-racks.

Wing span: approx 34·5 m (113 ft. 2 in.) to 26·25 m (86 ft. 1 in.)
Length: approx 40 m (131 ft. 2½ in.)
Max speed: approx Mach 1·9 or 2015 km/h (1255 mph)

Yak-36 Forger

The Yakovlev Yak-36 (NATO code-name Forger) is a VTOL combat aircraft operated from Soviet ASW carriers of the Kiev class. Its nose appears to house only a ranging radar, hence its use is probably limited to daylight air defence and light attack. It has two lift engines behind the cockpit, and a vectored-thrust engine farther aft.

Wing span: 7·32 m (24 ft. 0 in.)
Length: approx 15·25 m (5 ft. 0 in.)
Max speed: approx Mach 1·0 or 1060 km/h (661 mph)

71

Buccaneer

The British Aerospace Buccaneer was developed as a carrier-based strike aircraft for the RN. After the retirement of Britain's last conventional carrier, the Buccaneer was transferred to the RAF for land-based operations, but retained the wing-fold. It is also used by the South African Air Force.

Wing span: 12·9 m (42 ft. 4 in.)
Length: 19·33 m (63 ft. 5 in.)
Max speed: approx 955 km/h (595 mph)

Hawk

The British Aerospace Hawk was designed to be equally useful in both the pilot training and ground attack roles. All export Hawks have provisions for five weapon stations. Note the deep fuselage and moderately swept wing. A single-seat version is under development.

Wing span: 9·39 m (30 ft. 9¾ in.)
Length: 11·17 m (36 ft. 7¾ in.)
Max speed: 1038 km/h (658 mph)

Harrier GR3

Harrier GR3

The British Aerospace Harrier GR Mk 3 is the current RAF version of the world's first operational V/STOL combat aircraft. Though similar to the Sea Harrier, the GR3 is distinguished by its 'thimble' nose shape and flush canopy. the

Wing span: 7·7 m (25 ft. 3 in.)
Length: 13·89 m (45 ft 7 in.)
Max speed: 1175 km/h (735 mph)

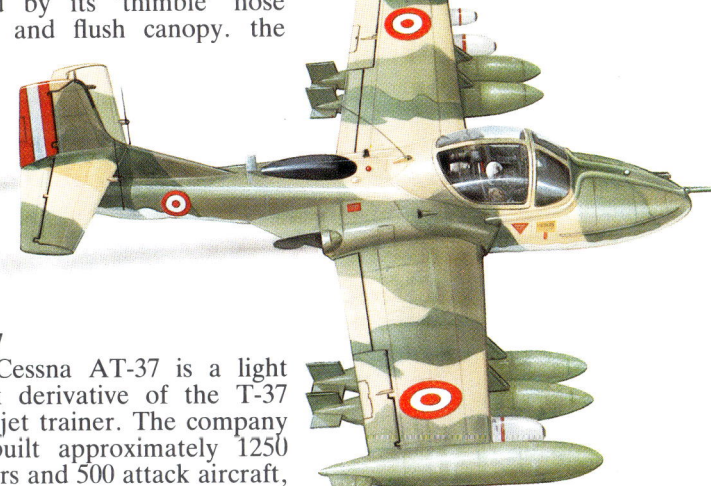

AT-37

The Cessna AT-37 is a light attack derivative of the T-37 basic jet trainer. The company has built approximately 1250 trainers and 500 attack aircraft, and it is now one of the most widely used of light military jets. Note the broad front fuselage and wing-root fairings for the two engines.

Wing span: 10·35 m (33 ft. 11½ in.)
Length: 8·93 m (29 ft. 3½ in.)
Max speed: 810 km/h (505 mph)

A-10A Thunderbolt II

The Fairchild Republic A-10A Thunderbolt II is a heavily armoured close support aircraft operated by the USAF, primarily for anti-tank duties. Relatively slow by jet standards, it relies on surviving (rather than avoiding) bullet strikes. The large, straight wing, twin fins and engine location are unmistakable.

Wing span: 17·53 m (57 ft. 6 in.)
Length: 16·26 m (53 ft. 4 in.)
Max speed: 705 km/h (440 mph)

73

B-52 Stratofortress

The Boeing B-52 Stratofortress is the world's largest bomber, but it is now very old. The type first flew in 1952, and in the following 10 years some 744 were built. The B-52 was used as a high level bomber in the Vietnam War. It remains in service as a cruise missile platform and for anti-ship duties.

Wing span: 56·40 m (185 ft. 0 in.)
Length: 48·04 m (157 ft. 6¾ in.)
Max speed: approx 955 km/h (595 mph)

F-16 Fighting Falcon

The General Dynamics F-16 Fighting Falcon was developed as a lightweight 'swing-force' fighter, which could be used in air superiority or ground attack, as the need arose. Due to its large internal fuel volume, it makes a good long-range strike aircraft, as the Israeli Air Force has demonstrated in attacking the Iraqi nuclear facility near Baghdad.

Wing span: 9·45 m (31 ft. 0 in.)
Length: 15·09 m (49 ft. 6 in.)
Max speed: over Mach 2·0 or 2120 km/h (1320 mph)

F-111

The General Dynamics F-111 is a swing-wing strike fighter with an all-weather capability. The first version (F-111A) saw active service in the Vietnam War between 1968 and 1973. The F-111A/D is now in service at two TAC bases in the US and two USAFE bases in England. The F-111C with extended wingtips is flown by the RAAF. The FB-111A with stretched wings and more powerful engines serves with SAC at two US bases.

Wing span: 19·21 m (63 ft. 0 in.) to 9·74 m (31 ft. 11½ in.)
Length: 22·4 m (73 ft. 5½ in.)
Max speed: Mach 2·5 or 2650 km/h (1650 mph)

A-6 Intruder

The Grumman A-6 Intruder is a twin-engined carrier-based attack aircraft, operated by the US Navy. Roughly equivalent to Britain's Buccaneer, the A-6 was used in the Vietnam War. The latest model is the A-6E with an infra-red sensor in a small ball turret under the nose.

Wing span: 16·15 m (53 ft. 0 in.)
Length: 16·69 m (54 ft. 9 in.)
Max speed: 1037 km/h (644 mph)

A-4 Skyhawk

The McDonnell Douglas A-4 Skyhawk had the longest production run of any US military aircraft, with 2960 built over a period of 26 years. Originally developed as a light attack aircraft for the US Navy and Marines, the A-4 was exported to eight countries, mainly for land-based operations. It served with distinction in Vietnam and several Middle East wars. The cropped delta wing and high tail are distinctive features.

Wing span: 8·38 m (27 ft. 6 in.)
Length: 12·29 m (40 ft. 3½ in.)
Max speed: approx 1120 km/h
  (700 mph)

AV-8B Harrier II

The McDonnell Douglas AV-8B Harrier II is a vastly improved derivative of the BAe Harrier, providing twice the warload or radius or action. In RAF service it will be known as the Harrier GR5. Note the enlarged wing, belly strakes and raised cockpit.

Wing span: 9·25 m (30 ft. 4 in.)
Length: 14·12 m (46 ft. 4 in.)
Max speed: 1095 km/h (685 mph)

B-1B

The Rockwell B-1B is a swing-wing heavy bomber, developed to supersede the B-52. Its design incorporates some 'stealth' technology, making it less vulnerable to radar detection. The B-1B will eventually be replaced by the Northrop Advanced Technology Bomber (ATB).

Wing span: 41·67 m (136 ft. 8½ in.) to 23·84 m (78 ft. 2½ in.)
Length: 44·81 m (147 ft. 0 in.)
Max speed: approx Mach 1·40 or 1485 km/h (925 mph)

A-7 Corsair II

The Vought A-7 Corsair II was designed to replace the much smaller A-4 in the light attack role. It served with the US Navy in the Vietnam War, but the USMC preferred to retain the A-4. The A-7 was later adopted by the USAF, but these aircraft have now been passed to ANG units. The chin intake and high, swept wing are two distinctive features.

Wing span: 11·8 m (38 ft. 9 in.)
Length: 14·06 m (46 ft. 1½ in.)
Max speed: 1105 km/h (690 mph)

Transport Aircraft

Buffalo

The de Havilland Canada DHC-5 Buffalo is an enlarged and more powerful derivative of the earlier DHC-4 Caribou. A STOL military transport, the Buffalo has the upswept rear fuselage that goes with a loading ramp. This eliminates the need for special ground facilities, enabling vehicles to be driven straight into the main cabin.

Wing span: 29·26 m (96 ft 0 in.)
Length: 24·08 m (79 ft. 0 in.)
Max cruise speed: 467 km/h (290 mph)

Transall

The Transall C-160 is a twin-engined tactical transport jointly developed by France and Germany. The first production batch was shared between those two air forces, and also South Africa and Turkey. A second batch is being constructed for France and Indonesia. The new French aircraft have refuelling probes over the cockpit, and some are equipped as tankers.

Wing span: 40 m (131 ft. 3 in.)
Length: 32·4 m (106 ft. 3½ in.)
Max cruise speed: 513 km/h (319 mph)

Arava

Arava

The Israel Aircraft Industries Arava is a twin-turboprop light tactical transport. It is used by the Israeli Air Force and a number of air forces in Africa, Asia and Latin America. Note the fixed undercarriage and twin booms, which allow the rear fuselage to be opened sideways for easy access to the cabin.

Wing span: 20·96 m (68 ft. 9 in.)
Length: 13·03 m (42 ft. 9 in.)
Max cruise speed: 319 km/h (198 mph)

G.222

The Aeritalia G.222 is similar in configuration to the Transall, but is a much smaller aircraft. The two can also be distinguished by their vertical tail shapes and cockpit transparencies, and by the lines of the lower rear fuselage. The G.222 also exists as an electronics warfare aircraft, with antennas under the nose and on the fin.

Wing span: 28·7 m (94 ft. 2 in.)
Length: 22·7 m (74 ft. 5½ in.)
Max cruise speed: 540 km/h (336 mph)

An-12 Cub

The Antonov An-12 (NATO code-name Cub) has been the standard transport and para-troop aircraft in the Soviet Air Force and several other air forces since about 1960. Most An-12s have a tail gun turret, which is deleted on later civil versions. The An-12 is also used for electronics warfare duties.

Wing span: 38·0 m (124 ft. 8 in.)
Length: 33·1 m (108 ft. 7½ in.)
Max cruise speed: 670 km/h (416 mph)

An-22 Cock

The Antonov An-22 (NATO code-name Cock) is a remarkably large transport aircraft. The Soviet Air Force is believed to operate around 50 examples, to move especially bulky loads such as main battle tanks. The An-22 holds a number of records for payload-to-height and speed-with-payload performance. Note the twin vertical tails.

Wing span: 64·4 m (211 ft. 4 in.)
Length: approx 58 m (190 ft. 3 in.)
Max cruise speed: 740 km/h (460 mph)

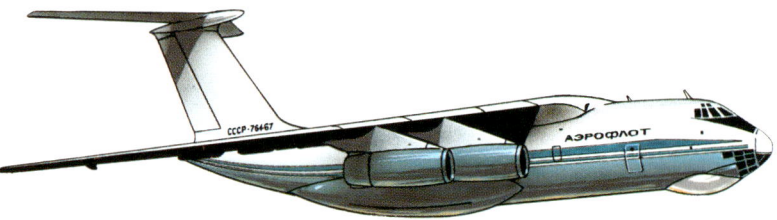

Il-76 Candid

The Ilyushin Il-76 (NATO code-name Candid) was developed as a replacement for the An-12. With swept wings and turbofan engines, it provided a major improvement in performance. It is used for both military and civil purposes, some military Il-76s having a tail gun turret. A tanker version is known to exist.

Wing span: 50·5 m (165 ft. 8 in.)
Length: 46·59 m (152 ft. 10½ in.)
Max cruise speed: 800 km/h (500 mph)

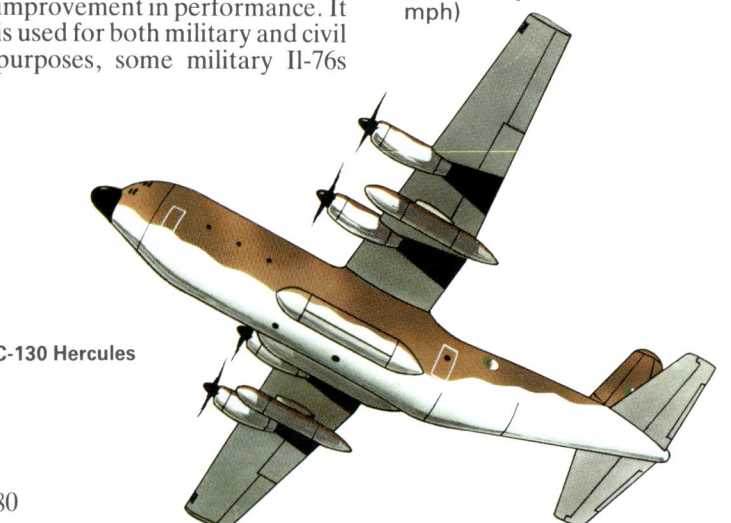

C-130 Hercules

C-130 Hercules

The Lockheed C-130 Hercules is probably the most widely used military transport aircraft in the world. It is powered by four turboprop engines, and is suitable for both medium and long ranges. Many different versions have been built, including tankers, and transport variants with a stretched cabin.

Wing span: 40·41 m (132 ft. 7 in.)
Length: 29·79 m (97 ft 9 in.)
Max cruise speed: 602 km/h (374 mph)

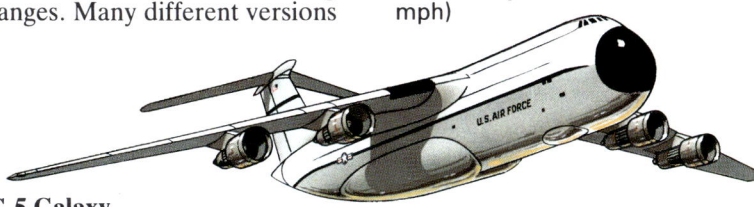

C-5 Galaxy

The Lockheed C-5 Galaxy is a heavy logistics transport aircraft, operated only by the USAF, which has 70 C-5As. A batch of 50 improved C-5Bs is now being built. The Soviet Union is developing a similar transport, code-named Condor.

Wing span: 67·88 m (222 ft. 8½ in.)
Length: 75·54 m (247 ft. 10 in.)
Max cruise speed: 908km/h (564 mph)

Maritime Patrol Aircraft

Atlantic

The Dassault-Breguet Atlantic is a twin-turboprop maritime patrol aircraft operated by France, Italy, the Netherlands and West Germany. A second generation Atlantic (ATL2) is now being produced for the French Navy, with a modernized equipment fit. The ATL2 may be distinguished by an infra-red sensor mounted under the nose.

Wing span: 37·42 m (122 ft. 9¼ in.)
Length: 33·63 m (110 ft. 4 in.)
Max cruise speed: 555 km/h (345 mph)

PS-1

The Shin Meiwa PS-1 is a Japanese ASW flying boat, operated by the JMSDF. The service also uses the PS-1 Mod amphibian for SAR duties. The hull is specially designed to permit open sea operation in quite high waves. One of the few flying boats still in use, the PS-1 series is unmistakable.

Wing span: 32·78 m (107 ft. 6½ in.)
Length: 33·5 m (109 ft. 11 in.)
Max cruise speed: 426 km/h (265 mph)

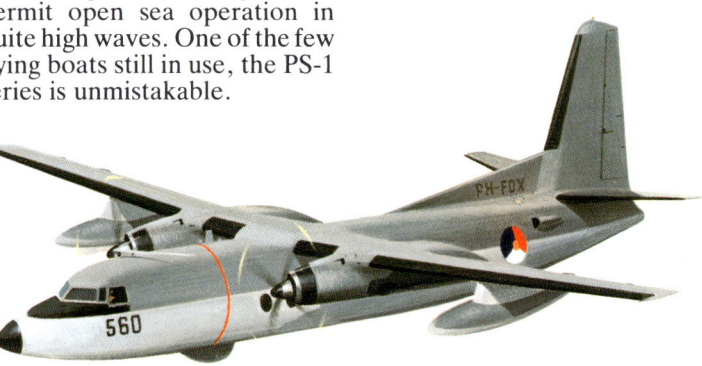

F27 Maritime

The Fokker F27 Maritime is a patrol version of the commercial F27 Friendship. Special equipment includes a belly-mounted radar and pylon-mounted fuel tanks. An armed version with six underwing pylons is known as the **Enforcer**. The Maritime is used by Angola, Iceland, the Netherlands, Peru, the Philippines, Spain and Thailand.

Wing span: 29·0 m (95 ft. 2 in.)
Length: 23·56 m (77 ft. 3½ in.)
Cruise speed: 463 km/h (287 mph)

Il-38 May

The Ilyushin Il-38 (NATO code-name May) is a maritime patrol and ASW derivative of the Il-18 commercial transport. It is distinguished from the airliner by its long tail 'sting' (for MAD equipment), the large radome under the front fuselage, and the small number of cabin windows. It is used by Soviet Naval Aviation and the Indian Navy.

Wing span: 37·4 m (122 ft. 8½ in.)
Length: 39·6 m (129 ft. 10 in.)
Max cruise speed: 645 km/h (400 mph)

Nimrod

The British Aerospace Nimrod MR Mk 2 is the standard RAF maritime patrol and ASW aircraft. It is the only aircraft in its class powered by four turbofan engines, which give high transit speeds to the search area. All MR2 are to have flight refuelling probes and provisions for Sidewinder AAMs and Harpoon anti-ship missiles.

Wing span: 35·0 m (114 ft. 10 in.)
Length: 38·63 m (126 ft. 9 in.)
Max cruise speed: 880 km/h (550 mph)

P-3C Orion

The Lockheed P-3C Orion is a maritime patrol derivative of the Electra four-turboprop airliner. It has a large nose radar and other sensors, including MAD equipment in a long tail 'sting'. The P-3 also has two weapon bays in the fuselage to house weapons, such as bombs, mines and torpedoes.

Wing span: 30·37 m (99 ft. 8 in.)
Length: 35·61 m (116 ft. 10 in.)
Max cruise speed: 760 km/h (473 mph)

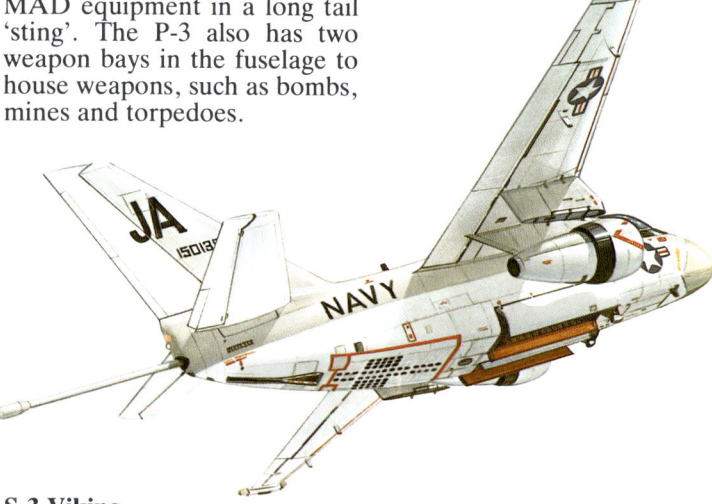

S-3 Viking

The Lockheed S-3 Viking is a carrier-based ASW aircraft operated by the US Navy. Some 187 S-3As were produced, and possible developments include tanker versions. The aircraft's high-set, slightly swept wing, large fin, and the closeness of the engines to the fuselage make it easy to recognize.

Wing span: 20·93 m (68 ft. 8 in.)
Length: 16·26 m (53 ft. 4 in.)
Max cruise speed: 649 km/h (403 mph)

84

Reconnaissance and Observation Aircraft

OV-1 Mohawk

The Grumman OV-1 Mohawk is a two-seat observation and reconnaissance aircraft operated by the US Army. It is often seen with a long SLAR pod under the front fuselage. Note the three vertical tails, the tadpole-shaped fuselage and the high-set turboprops.

Wing span: 12·8 m (42 ft. 0 in.)
Length: 12·5 m (41 ft. 0 in.)
Max speed: 491 km/h (305 mph)

TR-1A

The Lockheed TR-1A is a tactical reconnaissance version of the U-2 high-altitude strategic reconnaissance aircraft. It differs from the U-2 mainly in having special sensors, which allow it to look deep into enemy territory, without crossing the border. Probably the largest single-engined aircraft in the world, the U-2/TR-1 family is easily recognized.

Wing span: 31·39 m (103 ft. 0 in.)
Length: 19·2 m (63 ft. 0 in.)
Max cruise speed: 692 km/h (430 mph)

85

SR-71 Blackbird

The Lockheed SR-71A Blackbird is a high-speed, high altitude strategic reconnaissance aircraft, operated by SAC. The fastest production aircraft in service anywhere in the world, the SR-71A in 1976 established an absolute record of 3529·56 km/h (2193·17 mph), which stands today.

Wing span: 16·95 m (55 ft. 7 in.)
Length: 32·74 m (107 ft. 5 in.)
Max speed: approx Mach 3·3 or
3500 km/h (2185 mph)

OV-10 Bronco

The Rockwell OV-10 Bronco is a battlefield observation and forward air control (FAC) aircraft. Armament is normally carried on 'sponsons' attached to the centre fuselage. Cargo or troops may be carried in the rear fuselage. The latest version (OV-10D) has an infra-red sensor in the nose and provisions for a 20 mm gun turret under the fuselage.

Wing span: 12·19 m (40 ft. 0 in.)
Length: 13·41 m (44 ft. 0 in.)
Max speed: 463 km/h (288 mph)

Tankers

Tu-16 Badger

The Tupolev Tu-16 (NATO code-name Badger) is used by the Soviet armed forces as a tanker to refuel Tu-16 bombers and reconnaissance aircraft. An unusual method of refuelling is employed, in which a hose is passed from one wingtip of the tanker to the opposite tip of the receiver aircraft.

Wing span: 32·93 m (108 ft. 0 in.)
Length: 34·8 m (114 ft. 2 in.)
Max speed: approx 900 km/h (565 mph)

VC10

The British Aerospace VC10 K Mk 2 and Mk 3 tankers are conversions of civil VC10 and Super VC10 airliners. Hose-and-drogue type refuelling units in the fuselage and below the outer wing panels allow up to three aircraft to be refuelled simultaneously.

Wing span: 44·55 m (146 ft. 2 in.)
Length: (K3) 52·32 m (171 ft. 8 in.)
Max cruise speed: approx 910 km/h (568 mph)

87

KC-135 Stratotanker

The Boeing KC-135 Stratotanker still represents the backbone of the USAF tanker fleet. Some 732 were built, and approximately 650 remain in service. Small numbers have been exported. The USAF KC-135 uses the flying-boom method of transferring fuel, but some export aircraft have up to three hose-and-drogue units each.

Wing span: 39·89 m (130 ft. 10 in.)
Length: 41·54 m (136 ft. 3 in.)
Max cruise speed: approx 910 km/h (568 mph)

KC-10 Extender

The McDonnell Douglas KC-10A Extender is a tanker derivative of the DC-10-30CF convertible freighter aircraft. Modifications include the installation of fuel tanks in the lower fuselage, the deletion of most cabin windows, and the addition of a refuelling station in the lower rear fuselage. The KC-10 can use both boom and hose refuelling.

Wing span: 50·41 m (165 ft. 4½ in.)
Length: 55·35 m (181 ft. 7 in.)
Max cruise speed: 908 km/h (564 mph)

Airborne Early Warning Aircraft

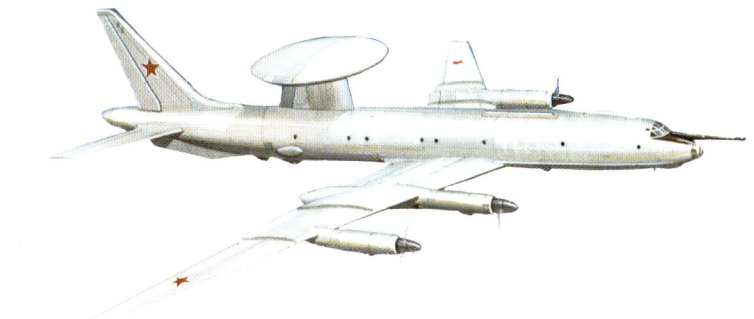

Tu-126 Moss

The Tupolev Tu-126 (NATO code-name Moss) is an AEW derivative of the Tu-114 four-turboprop airliner. The civil aircraft (rather than the Tu-95) was chosen as its basis, because of the much larger cabin this aircraft provided for avionics and crew. The large 'flying saucer' radome of the Tu-126 is said to give good results over water, but not over land.

Wing span: 51·2 m (168 ft. 0 in.)
Length: 55·2 m (181 ft. 1 in.)
Max speed: approx 850 km/h (530 mph)

Nimrod AEW3

The British Aerospace Nimrod AEW Mk 3 is an AEW conversion of the MR Mk 1. Some 11 aircraft are being modified for the RAF. The main external difference is the installation of large radomes in the nose and tail, giving radar coverage over the two hemispheres. The wing-tip pods sense external radar transmissions.

Wing span: 35·08 m (115 ft. 1 in.)
Length: 41·97 m (137 ft. 8½ in.)
Max cruise speed: approx 880 km/h (550 mph)

Sea King AEW

The Westland Sea King AEW helicopter is a conversion of the Mk2, which is used for ASW duties. The AEW version has a search radar in a 'kettledrum' radome, which is inflatable and retractable. For take-off and landing this radome is rotated upward and to the rear. The first conversions were made in 1982, in response to Britain's need for AEW capability in the South Atlantic.

Main rotor diameter: 18·9 m (62 ft. 0 in.)
Fuselage length: 17·01 m (55 ft. 9¾ in.)
Cruise speed: 208 km/h (129 mph)

E-3A Sentry

The Boeing E-3 Sentry is often referred to simply as AWACS (Airborne Warning and Control System). As this name implies, it provides not only an AEW facility, but also command and control capability. The E-3 is used by the USAF and NATO, and is on order for Saudi Arabia.

Wing span: 44·2 m (145 ft. 9 in.)
Length: 46·61 m (152 ft. 11 in.)
Max speed: 853 km/h (530 mph)

E-2C Hawkeye

The Grumman E-2 Hawkeye was originally developed as a carrier-based AEW aircraft, to replace the US Navy's E-1B Tracer. The E-1B had a fixed radome of aerofoil section, but the E-2 has a rotating 'flying saucer'. The E-2 was used during the Vietnam War, and was later sold to Egypt, Israel, Japan, and Singapore. Note the four fins, and the enlarged radiator behind the cockpit of the E-2C.

Wing span: 24·56 m (80 ft. 7 in.)
Length: 17·54 m (57 ft. 6¾ in.)
Max speed: 598 km/h (372 mph)

Electronic Warfare and Communications Aircraft

Il-20 Coot

The Ilyushin Il-20 (NATO code-name Coot) is a military version of the four-turboprop Il-18 airliner, with special equipment for electronic intelligence gathering. It has two large blade antennas on top of the front fuselage, two cylindrical bulges in the forward cabin sides, and a large cylindrical fairing under the fuselage, which probably houses further antennas.

Wing span: 37·4 m (122 ft. 8½ in.)
Length: 35.9 m (117 ft. 9 in.)
Max cruise speed: 675 km/h (419 mph)

EA-6B Prowler

The Grumman EA-6B Prowler is an EW derivative of the A-6 Intruder, with a longer front fuselage providing space for a crew of four. The Prowler is easily distinguished by its massive fin-tip radome, longer cockpit, and the four jammer pods that it often carries on underwing pylons. It is used by the US Navy and USMC.

Wing span: 16·15 m (53 ft. 0 in.)
Length: 18·24 m (59 ft. 10 in.)
Max speed: 1048 km/h (651 mph)

EF-111A Raven

The Grumman EF-111A Raven is an EW derivative of the General Dynamics F-111A. The EF-111A is distinguished from the earlier aircraft by its large fin-tip radome and the 'canoe' fairing under the fuselage, housing the jamming antennas.

Wing span: 19·21 m (63 ft. 0 in.) to 9·74 m (31 ft. 11¼ in.)
Length: 23·16 m (76 ft. 0 in.)
Max speed: Mach 2·15 or 2280 km/h (1420 mph)

E-4B

The Boeing E-4 AABNCP (Advanced Airborne Command Post) is a derivative of the 747-200B, intended to replace the EC-135. In war, the E-4 would maintain communications between US command centres and strategic retaliation forces, despite nuclear attacks. These aircraft could, for example, launch ICBMs, if ground control centres were destroyed.

Wing span: 59·64 m (195 ft. 8 in.)
Length: 70·51 m (231 ft. 4 in.)
Max speed: 970 km/h (605 mph)

Military Helicopters

SA 330 Puma

The Aérospatiale SA 330 Puma is one of three helicopter types jointly developed by the French company and Westland in the UK, the others being the Gazelle and Lynx. The Puma is a medium-size troop transport, though it is also used for civil purposes. It has now largely been superseded by the more powerful AS 332 Super Puma.

Main rotor diameter: 15 m (49 ft. 2½ in.)
Fuselage length: 14·06 m (46 ft. 1½ in.)
Max cruise speed: 271 km/h (168 mph)

SA 341/342 Gazelle

The Aérospatiale SA 341/342 Gazelle is a five-seat lightweight helicopter used for liaison and pilot training duties. The SA 342 has a more powerful engine than the 341. Some French Army Gazelles are armed with anti-tank guided missiles, and this lead has been followed by several export customers.

Main rotor diameter: 10·5 m (34 ft. 5½ in.)
Fuselage length: 9·53 m (31 ft. 3¼ in.)
Max cruise speed: 264 km/h (164 mph)

EH-101
The EH Industries EH-101 is a joint development by Britain's Westland and Italy's Agusta, aimed at producing a Sea King replacement. The EH-101 will be a three-engined helicopter, primarily used for ASW, anti-ship operations, SAR, and possibly AEW, resupply and EW. A civil version is also planned.

Main rotor diameter: 18·59 m (61 ft. 0 in.)
Length: 22·9 m (75 ft. 1¾ in.)
Max cruise speed: 278 km/h (173 mph)

A 129 Mangusta
The Agusta A 129 Mangusta (Mongoose) is a new Italian attack helicopter, designed to destroy armour in day/night all-weather conditions. The first prototype had its maiden flight on 15 September 1983. The launch customer is the Italian Army, which is expected to order a batch of 60.

Main rotor diameter: 11.9 m (39 ft. 0½ in.)
Fuselage length: 12·28 m (40 ft. 3¼ in.)
Max speed: 270 km/h (168 mph)

Ka-25 Hormone

The Kamov Ka-25 (NATO code-name Hormone) is the Soviet Navy's principal ASW helicopter, but it is also used for over-the-horizon targeting for ship-to-ship missiles, and for utility and SAR operations. Small numbers are also used by India, Syria and Yugoslavia. The contra-rotating main rotors eliminate the need for a tail rotor, and are used on other Kamov designs.

Main rotor diameter: 13 m (42 ft. 8 in.)
Fuselage length: 7·75 m (25 ft. 5 in.)
Max speed: 170 km/h (105 mph)

Mi-6 Hook

The Mil Mi-6 (NATO code-name Hook) is a heavy transport helicopter operated by the Soviet Air Force and by Algeria, Egypt, Ethiopia, Indonesia, Iraq, Peru, Syria and Vietnam. In its early days it was the world's largest helicopter. It still holds several records, including a 100 km circuit at 340·15 km/hr (211·36 mph), set in 1964.

Main rotor diameter: 35 m (114 ft. 10 in.)
Fuselage length: 33·18 m (108 ft. 10½ in.)
Max speed: 300 km/h (186 mph)

Mi-8 Hip

The Mil Mi-8 (NATO code-name Hip) is the standard Soviet assault transport helicopter. Unlike its Western counterparts, it is heavily armed, with guns, rockets and guided weapons. It is also in use in many overseas countries. The civil version has square windows to the cabin.

Main rotor diameter: 21·29 m (69 ft. 10½ in.)
Fuselage length: 18·17 m (59 ft. 7½ in.)
Max speed: 260 km/h (161 mph)

Mi-24 Hind

The Mil Mi-24 (NATO code-name Hind) is the standard Soviet attack helicopter, heavily armed with rockets, guns, and guided weapons. Unlike its Western counterpart (the Hughes AH-64), the Mi-24 has a cabin that can take eight fully armed troops. It is thought that the Mi-24 would also be used to attack other helicopters.

Main rotor diameter: 17 m (55 ft. 9 in.)
Length: 17·0 m (55 ft. 9 in.)
Max speed: 320 km/h (199 mph)

96

Sea King

The Westland Sea King is based on the airframe and rotor system of the Sikorsky SH-3D, but has British engines and systems to suit Royal Navy requirements. Its principal task is ASW, but other versions provide utility, SAR and AEW capabilities. The **Commando** is a special variant for land-based transport operations.

Main rotor diameter: 18·9 m (62 ft. 0 in.)
Fuselage length: 17·01 m (55 ft. 9¾ in.)
Cruise speed: 208 km/h (129 mph)

Lynx

The Westland Lynx was developed both as a general-purpose army helicopter and as a naval ASW system. In ground-based operations it is used as a troop transport and anti-tank helicopter. In the ASW role it has been accepted for frigate-based use in many NATO navies. The army version has skids and the navy version has wheels, which can be toed out to hold it firm on a wet, rolling deck.

Main rotor diameter: 12·8 m (42 ft. 0 in.)
Fuselage length: 12·06 m (39 ft. 6¾ in.)
Max cruise speed: 259 km/h (161 mph)

UH-1 Iroquois

The Bell UH-1 Iroquois (Model 205) was the principal US Army helicopter used in the Vietnam War. The 'Huey' was used both as an unarmed troop transport and as a gunship, pending the advent of the purpose-designed AH-1 HueyCobra. The series is still in production in Italy and Japan.

Main rotor diameter: 14·63 m (48 ft. 0 in.)
Fuselage length: 12·77 m (41 ft. 10¾ in.)
Max cruise speed: 204 km/h (127 mph)

OH-58D

The Bell OH-58D (Model 406) is the winner of the US Army AHIP (Army Helicopter Improvement Program), which was aimed at the development of an effective scout helicopter. The OH-58D will be produced by converting at least 578 existing OH-58A Kiowas, the military equivalent of the Model 206 JetRanger. It will be a two-seat aircraft with a four-blade rotor, a mast-mounted sighting system and provisions for air-to-air missiles.

Main rotor diameter: 10·67 m (35 ft. 0 in.)
Fuselage length: 10·31 m (33 ft. 10 in.)
Max speed: 237 km/h (147 mph)

AH-1 HueyCobra

The Bell AH-1 HueyCobra (Model 209) was developed as a 'dedicated' gunship during the Vietnam War, based on experience with the UH-1 series. The large cabin of the utility aircraft was replaced by a slender fuselage, seating the gunner and pilot in tandem. This arrangement also reduced drag, and the chances of the aircraft being seen and hit by enemy troops directly in front.

Main rotor diameter: 13·41 m (44 ft. 0 in.)
Fuselage length: 13·59 m (44 ft. 7 in.)
Max speed: 277 km/h (172 mph)

CH-46 Sea Knight

The Boeing Vertol CH-46 Sea Knight (Model 107) is a tandem-rotor assault transport helicopter, mainly used by the US Navy and USMC. It saw considerable service in Vietnam. The CH-46 can be distinguished from the later CH-47 by its small size, tricycle undercarriage and small sponsons.

Rotor diameter: 15·24 m (50 ft. 0 in.)
Fuselage length: 13·67 m (44 ft. 10 in.)
Max speed: 246 km/h (154 mph)

CH-47 Chinook

The Boeing Vertol CH-47 Chinook (Model 114 and export 414) is a medium transport helicopter, developed for the US Army. It saw limited use in Vietnam. The tandem-rotor arrangement was largely developed by Piasecki, the forerunner of Vertol. Like the CH-46, the Chinook has a rear loading ramp. Note the four undercarriage units and the long sponsons, which contain fuel.

Rotor diameter: 18·29 m (60 ft. 0 in.)
Fuselage length: 15·54 m (51 ft. 0 in.)
Max speed: 291 km/h (181 mph)

Hughes 500MD

The Hughes 500MD Defender is a military derivative of the civil Model 500, with armament provisions, optional armour, self-sealing fuel tanks, a Hughes 'Black Hole' IR suppression system, and other changes. The 500MD can carry the TOW (Tube launched, Optically tracked, Wire Guided) anti-tank missile; this version has been bought by Israel, Kenya and South Korea.

Main rotor diameter: 8·05 m (26 ft. 4¾ in.)
Fuselage length: 7·01 m (23 ft. 0 in.)
Max cruise speed: 221 km/h (137 mph)

AH-64 Apache

The Hughes AH-64 Apache was developed to meet a US Army requirement for an Advanced Attack Helicopter (AAH), capable of day/night all-weather operations. It has a two-man crew sitting in tandem with the gunner in front. The nose contains a night vision and laser designation system. Armament includes Hellfire missiles and a Hughes 30 mm Chain Gun mounted under the fuselage.

Main rotor diameter: 14·63 m (48 ft. 0 in.)
Length overall: 17·76 m (58 ft. 3¼ in.)
Max cruise speed: 293 km/h (182 mph)

SH-2 Seasprite

The Kaman SH-2 Seasprite is the basis for the US Navy's Mk 1 LAMPS (Light Airborne Multi-Purpose System). Its principal roles are to provide ASW and anti-ship surveillance and targeting. In ASW operations it is normally seen with a light-weight torpedo on the left side and a MAD 'dart' on the right. It has a tricycle undercarriage, of which the tailwheel does not retract.

Main rotor diameter: 13·41 m (44 ft. 0 in.)
Length: 16·03 m (52 ft. 7 in.)
Max speed: 265 km/h (165 mph)

101

Super Stallion

The Sikorsky CH-53E/MH-53E Super Stallion is an enlarged three-engined derivative of the twin-engined CH-53D Stallion. The amphibious assault CH-53E takes up to 55 Marines.

Main rotor diameter: 24·08 m (79 ft. 0 in.)
Fuselage length: 22·35 m (73 ft. 4 in.)
Max speed: 315 km/h (196 mph)

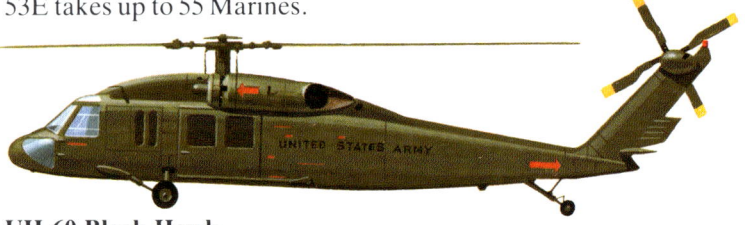

UH-60 Black Hawk

The Sikorsky UH-60 Black Hawk was developed to meet a US Army requirement for a new tactical transport helicopter to replace the UH-1. It can carry 11 fully equipped troops, and there are provisions for externally mounted stores, including fuel tanks and guided missiles.

The USAF has a requirement for a rescue version, designated HH-60 Night Hawk.

Main rotor diameter: 16·36 m (53 ft. 8 in.)
Fuselage length: 15·26 m (50 ft. 0¾ in.)
Max speed: 296 km/h (184 mph)

SH-60 Sea Hawk

The Sikorsky SH-60B Sea Hawk is a derivative of the UH-60, designed to fulfil a US Navy requirement (LAMPS Mk III) for an ASW and anti-ship surveillance and targeting helicopter. The SH-60 will serve on a variety of destroyers, cruisers and guided missile frigates. The tailwheel has been brought forward to allow a tail fold.

Main rotor diameter: 16·36 m (53 ft. 8 in.)
Folded length: 12·47 m (40 ft. 11 in.)
Max speed: 269 km/h (167 mph)

Prop-driven Trainers

A10

The Australian Aircraft Consortium (AAC) A10 is a turboprop trainer designed to replace the CT4A piston-engined primary trainer in RAAF service. It is unusual in being the only one of its class to have side-by-side seating. A tandem-seat version designated A20 has been proposed to meet RAF demands for a Jet Provost replacement.

Wing span: 11 m (36 ft. 1 in.)
Length: 10·01 m (32 ft. 10 in.)
Max cruise speed: 333 km/h (207 mph)

EMB-312 Tucano

The Embraer EMB-312 Tucano (Toucan) is a tandem-seat turboprop trainer, designed to meet Brazilian Air Force needs for a basic trainer (designated T-27). The Tucano is unusual in having been designed from the outset to have ejection seats, possibly with an eye on counter-insurgency operations.

Wing span: 11·14 m (36 ft. 6½ in.)
Length: 9·86 m (32 ft. 4¼ in.)
Max cruise speed: 441 km/h (274 mph)

103

L-70 Vinka

The Valmet L-70 Vinka (Blast) is a Finnish piston-engined primary trainer, of which 30 have been built for the Finnish Air Force. Typical of aircraft in this class, it has a fixed tricycle undercarriage. The L-70 has been offered for export with the name Miltrainer. A turboprop derivative, the L-80TP, is being developed.

Wing span: 9·63 m (31 ft. 7¼ in.)
Length: 7·5 m (24 ft. 7¼ in.)
Max speed: 235 km/h (146 mph)

Epsilon

The Aérospatiale Epsilon is a high-powered piston-engined primary trainer, in service with the French Air Force (150 aircraft on order). It has a retractable undercarriage and a tall, distinctive vertical tail. An armed version is offered for export.

Wing span: 7·92 m (25 ft. 11¾ in.)
Length: 7·59 m (24 ft. 10¾ in.)
Max speed: 380 km/h (236 mph)

Fantrainer

The Rhein-Flugzeugbau (RFB) Fantrainer is a tandem-seat basic trainer, being manufactured in Germany for the Royal Thai Air Force. It is unique in having a turbine engine in the centre fuselage, driving a ducted fan. This arrangement is clearly safer (and may be quieter) than a conventional propeller. Note the slight forward sweep of the wing and the high tail.

Wing span: 9·7 m (31 ft. 10 in.)
Length: 9·23 m (30 ft. 3½ in.)
Max speed: 430 km/h (267 mph)

SF.260

The Siai-Marchetti SF.260 is one of the most successful piston-engined primary trainers, with over 800 sold for military and civil use. It has a retractable undercarriage, side-by-side seating, tip tanks, and a slightly swept fin. A turboprop version (SF.260TP) has been sold in small numbers.

Wing span: 8·35 m (27 ft. 4¾ in.)
Length: 7·1 m (23 ft. 3½ in.)
Max speed: 333 km/h (207 mph)

105

PC-7

The Pilatus PC-7 is a turboprop derivative of the piston-engined P-3. One of the most successful aircraft in its class, the PC-7 is used both for primary/basic training and close support duties. An improved version, the PC-9, with increased power, a raised rear seat and many refinements is under development. The Mustang-like vertical tail makes the PC-7 easy to recognize.

Wing span: 10·4 m (34 ft. 1½ in.)
Length: 9·78 m (32 ft. 0¾ in.)
Max cruise speed: 412 km/h (256 mph)

Yak-52

The Yakovlev Yak-52 is a radial-engined, tandem-seat primary trainer, designed to replace the Yak-18 in Soviet Air Force service. It is now being built in Romania. The under-carriage is semi-retractable, the wheels projecting down from the wings and fuselage when the legs are raised. The radial engine, long 'glasshouse' and curved fin are good recognition points.

Wing span: 9·3 m (30 ft. 6¼ in.)
Length: 7·75 m (25 ft. 5 in.)
Max speed: 300 km/h (186 mph)

NDN-1T Firecracker

The NDN Aircraft NDN-1T Turbo-Firecracker is a turbo-prop version of the earlier piston-engined Firecracker. The series is easily recognized by its un-usual short-span wing, which is intended to provide handling characteristics like those of an operational combat aircraft.

Wing span: 7·92 m (26 ft. 0 in.)
Length: 8·33 m (27 ft. 4 in.)
Max speed: 420 km/h (261 mph)

T-34C Turbine Mentor

The Beech T-34C Turbine Men-tor is a turboprop development of the piston-engined T-34B. It is used by the US Navy as a basic trainer and by several export customers either for pilot train-ing or light attack duties. The angular fin and underside strake are easily recognized.

Wing span: 10·16 m (33 ft. 3¾ in.)
Length: 8·75 m (28 ft. 8½ in.)
Max cruise speed: 396 km/h (246 mph)

Jet Trainers

IA-63

The Fábrica Militar de Aviones (FMA) IA-63 (reported to be named *Pampa*), is a straight-wing tandem-seat basic jet trainer, designed by FMA in co-operation with Dornier. In Argentine service it will replace the MS.760 Paris.

Wing span: 9·67 m (31 ft. 9 in.)
Length: 10·93 m (35 ft. 10¼ in.)
Max speed: 740 km/h (460 mph)

L-39 Albatros

The Aero L-39 Albatros is a Czech basic jet trainer, which is employed by most Warsaw Pact air forces and several other military operators. It is described as the first of the new generation of turbofan-powered trainers, having first flown in 1968. It is also used for target towing and light attack duties.

Wing span: 9·46 m (31 ft. 0½ in.)
Length: 12·13 m (39 ft. 9½ in.)
Max speed: 755 km/h (469 mph)

Alpha Jet

The Dassault-Breguet/Dornier Alpha Jet is used by the French Air Force and some export customers as an advanced trainer. The trainer differs from the Luftwaffe ground attack version in having a rounded nose with strakes, which give consistent spinning behaviour. This nose is retained in the case of dual-role export aircraft.

Wing span: 9·11 m (29 ft. 10¾ in.)
Length: 12·29 m (40 ft. 3¾ in.)
Max speed: 1040 km/h (645 mph)

MB-326

The Aermacchi MB-326 was the most successful basic jet trainer outside the Warsaw Pact countries and the US, with almost 800 built. It is distinguished from the later MB-339 by the fact that the rear cockpit is raised very little relative to that in front.

Wing span: 10·03 m (32 ft. 10¾ in.)
Length: 10·67 m (35 ft. 0 in.)
Max speed: 800 km/h (500 mph)

MB-399

The Aermacchi MB-339 is a derivative of the earlier MB-326, with a more powerful engine, stronger structure, and many refinements. It is distinguished from the MB-326 by the depth of the front fuselage. A single-seat version, the MB-339K Veltro 2, with built-in cannon, has also been developed.

Wing span: 10·86 m (35 ft. 7½ in.)
Length: 10·97 m (36 ft. 0 in.)
Max speed: 898 km/h (558 mph)

S.211

The Siai-Marchetti S.211 is the first of a new generation of basic trainers, combining the fuel efficiency of turbofan engines developed for business jet use, and the aerodynamic benefits of a 'supercritical' wing. Note the high wing and relatively fat fuselage.

Wing span: 8·43 m (27 ft. 8 in.)
Length: 9·31 m (30 ft. 6½ in.)
Max speed: 667 km/h (414 mph)

TS-11 Iskra

The PZL TS-11 Iskra (Spark) is Poland's basic jet trainer, which is also operated by the Indian Air Force. The 'pod-and-boom' layout of the fuselage is distinctive. There is also a single-seat reconnaissance version, and reports of a development with a turbofan engine similar to that of the L-39.

Wing span: 10·06 m (33 ft. 0 in.)
Length: 11·15 m (36 ft. 7 in.)
Max speed: 770 km/h (478 mph)

Hawk

The British Aerospace Hawk advanced trainer and ground attack aircraft was designed to replace the Gnat in RAF service, and to supersede aircraft such as the Hunter in the export market. A single-seat version (200-series) is under development, as is a navalized version (T-45A) for the US Navy. The T-45A is capable of landing and taking off from aircraft carriers, with twin nosewheels, an arrester hook, and twin airbrakes.

Wing span: 9·39 m (30 ft. 9¾ in.)
Length: 11·17 m (36 ft. 7¾ in.)
Max speed: 1038 km/h (645 mph)

T-46

The Fairchild Republic T-46A was the winner in the USAF NGT (next generation trainer) contest to replace the T-37 basic jet trainer. It goes against the general trend, in having side-by-side seating. Note the high wing, rather square intakes and twin fins (for good spin recovery), An armed export version is designated FRC-225 or AT-46.

Wing span: 11·27 m (36 ft. 11¾ in.)
Length: 8·99 m (29 ft. 6 in.)
Max speed: 741 km/h (460 mph)

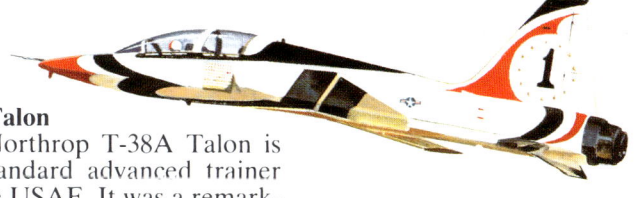

T-38 Talon

The Northrop T-38A Talon is the standard advanced trainer for the USAF. It was a remarkable design in its day, combining lightweight engines and the use of Area Rule to achieve supersonic speed in a very small aircraft. The T-38 also has one of the finest safety records for military jet aircraft.

Wing span: 7·7 m (25 ft. 3 in.)
Length: 14·13 m (46 ft. 4 in.)
Max speed: Mach 1·30 or 1370 km/h (860 mph)

G-4 Super Galeb

The Soko G-4 Super Galeb (Seagull) might be described as Yugoslavia's answer to Italy's MB-339. It uses the same type of engine, but it has a slightly swept wing, apparently giving a small advantage in speed. The G-4 is also much higher off the ground, and has provisions for a centre-line 23 mm cannon pod.

Wing span: 9·88 m (32 ft. 5 in.)
Length: 11·86 m (38 ft. 11 in.)
Max speed: 910 km/h (565 mph)

Civil Aircraft Today

The problems and decisions facing the designers of commercial transport aircraft are quite different from those that designers of combat aircraft have to deal with. Commercial airliner designers are more concerned with the precise demands of the market and with operating costs. They have to judge the relative claims of different engine manufacturers – for in this highly competitive market tiny changes in fuel consumption may mean success or failure.

How Many Engines?
Sometimes the number of engines on an aircraft is dictated by what types of powerplant are available. The designers of the BAe 146 regional transport wanted to produce a plane which was quieter and burned less fuel than the existing Fokker F28. This meant that they had to find an advanced high-bypass turbofan engine. As the only suitable engine on the market at the time was relatively small, a four-engined aircraft was called for.

Regional transport planes, which are airliners intended for services within an area such as Europe or the USA, generally have two or three engines. Recently, following the success of the Boeing 737 and Douglas DC-9 series, the trend has been in favour of twin-engined aircraft. Twin-engined aircraft now benefit in safety from the reliability of modern turbofans.

The twin-engined airliner has a very good safety record, but it is not suitable for extremely long flights across water. This is because it has to be able to divert to a suitable airfield within a fixed time of one engine failing. If an engine develops a serious fault at an airport remote from the airline's maintenance base, the engine must be repaired or replaced on the spot. The aircraft cannot return to base with one engine inoperative, in the way that the four-engined BAe 146 could. A three- or four-engined aircraft is also at an advantage in mountainous regions, as a loss of power on one engine affects its cruise altitude far less than it would that of a twin. The designers of twin-engined aircraft have to ensure that it can meet the requirements of take-off and climb, even if one engine fails. This means that it tends to be overpowered.

◀ **The Embraer EMB-110P1 Bandeirante**
air ambulance in the insignia of the
Instituto Mexicano de Seguro Social.

ENGINE ARRANGEMENT

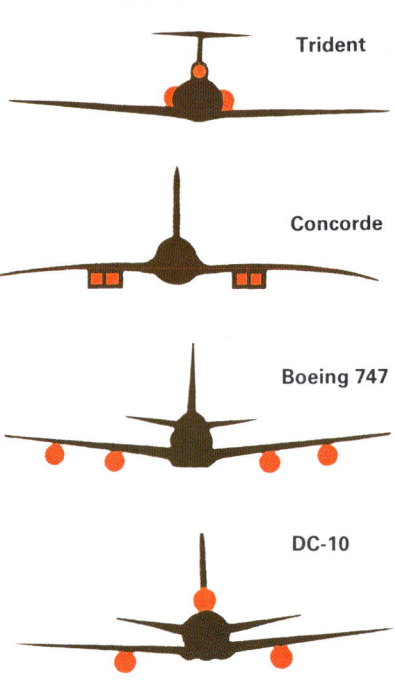

Trident

Concorde

Boeing 747

DC-10

Positioning the Engines

The first of the twin-jet regional transports was the Sud (later Aerospatiale) Caravelle, which went into production in the early 1950s. The Caravelle introduced the idea of having the engines mounted on rear fuselage pylons. One advantage of this arrangement was that it gave a quiet cabin, as the engines were well behind it. It also put the air intakes above any spray that might splash up from the nose wheels in wet conditions. This layout also meant that an engine failure

produced little tendency to yaw to one side.

The Caravelle engine layout was to have great impact on airline design in the years that followed. It was adopted by the designers of the BAC One-Eleven and DC-9 and by most of the business jets. But the arrangement does have certain disadvantages; it tends to produce a far heavier structure than the alternative layout with the engines under the wings. Another possible drawback is that it forces the designer to adopt the T-tail arrangement, which can lead to a 'superstall' problem. In the 'superstall' situation the stalled wing 'blankets' the horizontal tail and makes recovery impossible. Many T-tail aircraft have to have devices to prevent this arising.

Other twin-engined airliners, such as the Boeing 737, have a different arrangement with the engines under the wings. This is more efficient structurally, since it reduces wing bending loads and allows a lighter rear fuselage. Because the engines are nearer the ground they are more accessible. But the vertical tail needs to be larger to counter yaw in the event of engine failure and the proximity of the engine intakes to the ground may allow them to pick up debris.

The first airliners to adopt the three-engine arrangement were the DH Trident and

Boeing 727, which had all the engines at the rear, with the centre one buried in the aft fuselage. On the wide-bodied Lockheed L-1011 TriStar the two outer engines were moved to the wings, but the central engine was kept inside the fuselage. The McDonnell Douglas DC-10 has a similar arrangement but has the central engine buried in the vertical tail, giving a straight line intake duct rather than an S-bend. This must make the central engine rather inaccessible, but modern engines are so reliable that it does not appear to be a severe disadvantage.

Wings – High and Low

The wing of a high performance airliner is generally placed fairly low on the fuselage. This is partly the result of pressurization. To enable passengers to breathe in the rarified atmosphere of high altitudes, the fuselage of a passenger plane has to be pressurized – pumped full of air. To stand up to the force of pressurization the aircraft has to be strongly built

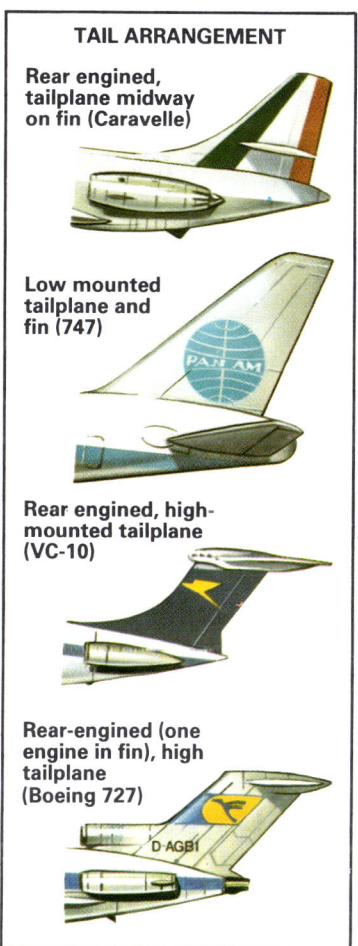

TAIL ARRANGEMENT

Rear engined, tailplane midway on fin (Caravelle)

Low mounted tailplane and fin (747)

Rear engined, high-mounted tailplane (VC-10)

Rear-engined (one engine in fin), high tailplane (Boeing 727)

and the fuselage should be roughly circular in cross-section. The most convenient way of using this circular shape is by placing the passengers in the upper part and the freight underneath. The main wing structure has to pass through the fuselage and it is more acceptable to take it through the freight hold than through the passenger cabin. A medium low wing is therefore the natural choice for a large airliner intended mainly for passenger operations. In this arrangement the cabin floor is high off the ground, which could in theory make it difficult for passengers to get on and off. Some aircraft, such as the Caravelle, 727 and One-Eleven,

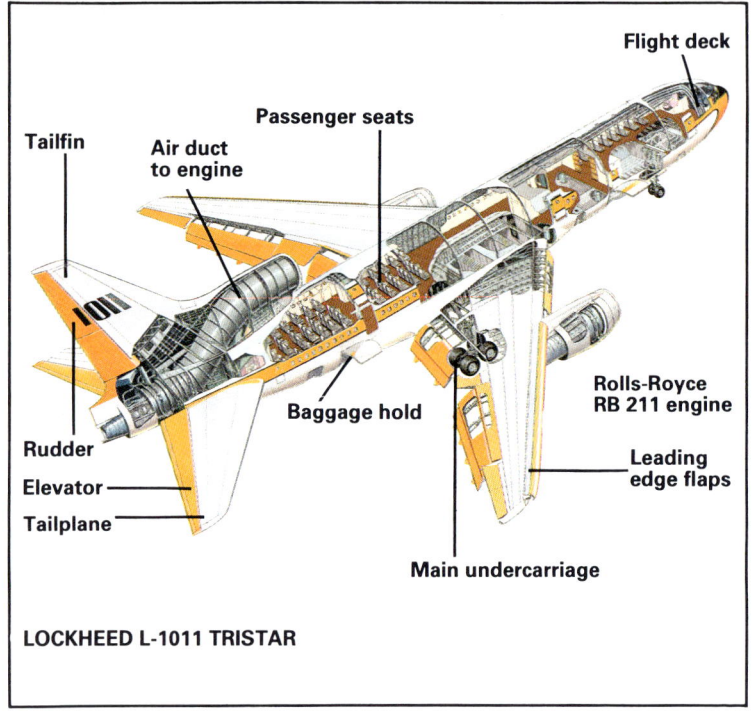

Flight deck

Passenger seats

Tailfin

Air duct to engine

Rolls-Royce RB 211 engine

Baggage hold

Rudder

Elevator

Tailplane

Leading edge flaps

Main undercarriage

LOCKHEED L-1011 TRISTAR

have built-in airstairs, but they are seldom required in jet airliners. Most major airports have special facilities to ease problems of passenger loading.

The low wing gives a clean wing-body juncture. An aerodynamically clean aircraft is important in this class of transport, since it has to cruise economically at high speeds over long distances.

The requirements on short routes are different from those on long international routes. Passengers will not be so concerned about speed, but they will expect flights to be more frequent. Somebody travelling from London to Sydney is probably quite happy with a choice of two departure times a day. Someone travelling from London to Manchester expects an hourly service. On these short routes the operator may choose a relatively slow turboprop transport.

The small, slow airliner will probably still have a circular-section fuselage to suit pressurization loads. The passenger cabin will take up most of the cross-section and there will be a small underfloor freight hold. In this case, the obvious approach is to take the wing

▲ **Three Embraer aeroplanes**. From top to bottom: the Brasilia, the Bandeirante and the Xingu.

structure over the top of the cabin. A large 'fairing' (a streamlined shape) will blend the wing and the fuselage together. This is not as elegant aerodynamically as the low wing used on larger transports, but the short-range aircraft is less sensitive to drag.

One advantage of the high wing arrangement is that it places the cabin floor close to ground level. The small, light airstairs can be easily stowed away inside the airliner, without any serious weight penalty. The aircraft is also able to operate from small airfields with limited facilities. Another advantage of the high wing is that it lifts the engine well clear of the ground. This means that the intakes are less likely to pick up dust and debris, which can be a particular problem in desert regions. The F27, BAe 146, Dash-8 and ATR-42 are all examples of the high-wing airliner. But not all manufacturers of small airliners favour the high wing. The manufacturers of the Brasilia and the SF-340, for instance, have opted for a low wing because of the better cruise performance that this layout provides.

A high wing tends to cause a long, 'stalky' undercarriage, which makes it less suitable for rough airstrips. This problem can be overcome by mounting the undercarriage on the fuselage, as is the case on the C-212 and CN-235. This also makes the aircraft more suitable for use in military operations, in combination with a rear-loading ramp.

▲ **The Dassault-Breguet Falcon 10** 'mini-Falcon', the smallest in the range of business jets produced by this French manufacturer.

Commuters and 'Bizjets'

Small commuter aircraft are normally used on short flights. This means that they tend not to fly at very high altitudes and therefore do not require pressurization. Visibility from the aircraft's windows is a particularly important design consideration when a plane is to be used at fairly low levels. A high wing provides a far better view when the aircraft is flying level, although the view tends to be lost in turns. High-wing aircraft in this category include the Twin Otter, Do 228 and An-28. The Bandeirante, Jetstream and Beech 1900, on the other hand, all have the wing set low.

The design requirements of business jets are quite different. These small aircraft have very high speed and long range for their size. Clean aerodynamics favours a low wing, which in turn dictates a Caravelle-type engine installation in the rear fuselage – the wing is too close to the ground to have engines underneath. Of the first generation 'bizjets', the Citation I was designed for short field performance. In order to achieve high performance at a relatively low cost, the manufacturers of the early Learjets made the diameter of the cabin rather small. On the Falcon 200 high performance was achieved through a large wing-sweep angle, which compensated for the much larger cabin. On the BAe 125 the wing structure passes below the pressure cabin to give the maximum possible height for a given fuselage diameter.

118

The present trend appears to be to increase the speed, range and cabin diameter of business jets. Aircraft such as the Challenger, Gulfstream, and Falcon 900 represent a superlative way to travel, for those fortunate enough to be able to afford them. In the longer term it seems that many of the current smaller bizjets will be replaced by advanced turboprops. Over short stages this new generation will be just as fast as present-day jets, and will provide much lower operating costs.

Smaller Aircraft
The smaller aircraft in the general aviation field have seen few major changes during the past few decades. But advanced wing sections are now being introduced and composite materials are being used more widely in their airframes. There is also a move to replace piston engines with turboprops, which are smoother and probably more reliable, although far more expensive.

Agricultural aircraft represent a special design case. They are usually single-engined. This is the most dangerous form of aviation, since agricultural aircraft spend most of their flying lives close to the ground in crop-dusting and spraying operations. They tend to fly into trees and high tension cables. The designer has to give the pilot the best possible forward view, and the best possible chance of surviving an impact with obstacles or the ground.

▼ **A Bell Model 412** helicopter in use as off-shore oil support.

▲ **A sailplane** glides high above its airfield.

A low wing is an advantage in a crash situation, and it is generally safer to place the pilot behind and above the mass of the hopper that contains the chemicals. The pilot is given an extremely strong seat and harness, and a pylon behind his head to protect him if the aircraft crashes upside down. The fuel tanks are sometimes placed in the outer wings, to keep the fire risks as far as possible from the pilot.

Sailplanes are another special case, aimed at achieving the highest possible level of aerodynamic refinement in order to attain excellent gliding performance. For this reason the sailplane has a wing that is very broad (from tip to tip) in relation to its chord. This reduces the drag associated with wing lift. The combined effect of this wing shape, a very slender fuselage (the pilot almost lying on his back) and a very smooth surface finish is that the sailplane can generate an aerodynamic lift of around 40 times its drag. A subsonic transport aircraft has a best lift/drag ratio of around 18, and a fighter may reach perhaps 12.

Lightweight turbine engines have benefited rotary-wing aircraft particularly. This is because VTO performance depends critically on the weight of the aircraft when empty. The vast majority of civil helicopters use the same configuration, with a single main rotor. Helicopters also have a tail rotor to prevent the main rotor rotating the aircraft, and to provide yaw control. Composite materials are being used to make the blades last longer and the shape of the blades is gradually being improved.

Into the Future

The next important step in the development of commercial aviation will be the advent of a new type of powerplant, giving significant fuel economies without losing high cruise speed capability. The 'propfan' may be seen as a compromise between the turboprop and the turbofan, or (alternatively) as a turboprop with an unusually large number of small-diameter blades. If the propfan is to be installed efficiently, the designer should avoid placing it in a position where it will expose a large area of wing to its high-energy slipstream. The effect of this would be to increase drag. It may be that the propfan is best installed at the rear of the aircraft, rather like the jet engines of the Caravelle.

Other possible lines of development include long-range supersonic transports, able to fly from Europe to the US West Coast non-stop. The growing market for specialized freight aircraft may also justify new designs of novel configuration. The threatened rise of conventional fuel prices may force the use of alternative fuels, such as liquid hydrogen, which will require massive pressurized and insulated tanks. Nuclear-powered aircraft have been talked of for many years, although their application seems more likely to be on the military side.

▼ **The Boeing 767** in the livery of Ethiopian Airlines.

Airline Liveries

**Aer Lingus
(Republic of
Ireland)**

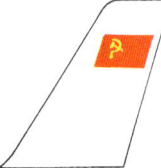

**Aeroflot
(Soviet Union)**

**Canada
(Canada)**

**Air France
(France)**

**Air-India
(India)**

**Air Malta
(Malta)**

**Alitalia
(Italy)**

**Braathens-SAFE
(Norway)**

**British Airways
(United Kingdom)**

**British Caledonian
(United Kingdom)**

**Cathay Pacific
(Hong Kong)**

**CP Air
(Canada)**

**CSA
(Czechoslovakia)**

**El Al
(Israel)**

**Gulf Air
(Oman)**

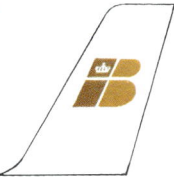

**Iberia
(Spain)**

**Interflug
(East Germany)**

**Iraqi Airways
(Iraqi)**

**Japan Air Lines
(Japan)**

**KLM
(Netherlands)**

**LOT
(Poland)**

**Lufthansa
(West Germany)**

**Pan Am
(United States)**

**Qantas
(Australia)**

**Sabena
(Belgium)**

**SAS
(Denmark, Norway,
Sweden)**

**Saudia
(Saudia Arabia)**

**South African
Airlines
(South Africa)**

**Swissair
(Switzerland)**

**TWA
(United States)**

**Varig
(Brazil)**

**World Airways
(United States)**

Airliners (100 seats and over)

Concorde

A300

The Airbus Industrie A300 is a wide-body airliner with a swept wing and two large turbofan engines. A joint development by Britain, France, the Netherlands, Spain and West Germany, the A300 is a highly successful medium-haul transport. The A310 is a short-body derivative, and the A300-600 is a slightly stretched version.

Wing span: 44·84 m (147 ft. 1 in.)
Length: 53·62 m (175 ft. 11 in.)
Passengers: 220–320
Cruise speed: 847–911 km/h (526–567 mph)

Tu-154 Careless

The Tupolev Tu-154 (NATO code-name Careless) is a medium/long-range airliner with three turbofan engines, arranged in a similar fashion to those of the Trident and Boeing 727. The characteristic Tupolev wing fairings over the main undercarriage are distinctive.

Wing span: 37·55 m (123 ft. 2½ in.)
Length: 47·9 m (157 ft. 1¾ in.)
Passengers: 144–168
Cruise speed: 900–950 km/h (560–590 mph)

Concorde

Concorde is the world's most advanced airliner, a joint product of British Aerospace and Aerospatiale. Flying at twice the speed of sound, it halves flight times across the North Atlantic. Its slender delta wing and the sound of its afterburning engines are unmistakable.

Wing span: 25·61 m (84 ft. 0 in.)
Length: 62·2 m (204 ft. 0 in.)
Passengers: 100–144
Cruise speed: Mach 2·02 or 2140 km/h (1335 mph)

Il-62 Classic

The Ilyushin Il-62 (NATO code-name Classic) is a long-range airliner of similar configuration to Britain's VC10, with four turbofan engines mounted on the sides of the rear fuselage. The Il-62 can be recognized by its wing leading edge extensions, taller fin, square-cut tail-plane, and the larger fairing at the tail intersection.

Wing span: 43·2 m (141 ft. 9 in.)
Length: 52·12 m (174 ft. 3½ in.)
Passengers: 114–186
Cruise speed: 820–900 km/h (510–560 mph)

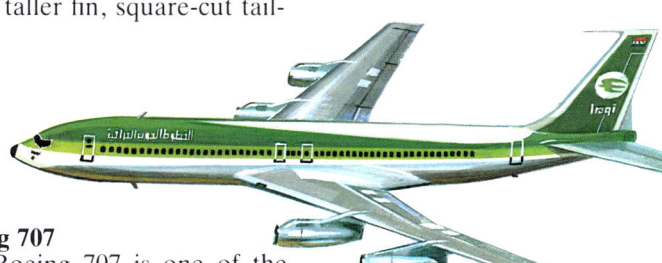

Boeing 707

The Boeing 707 is one of the great classic airliners, which in the late 1950s brought jet speeds to all the major long-range routes. The swept wing with four underslung engines was followed by the Douglas DC-8. The 707 can be recognized by its nose shape and vertical tail, carrying an air data probe.

Wing span: 44·42 m (145 ft. 9 in.)
Length: 46·61 m (152 ft. 11 in.)
Passengers: 130–219
Cruise speed: 850–973 km/h (530–605 mph)

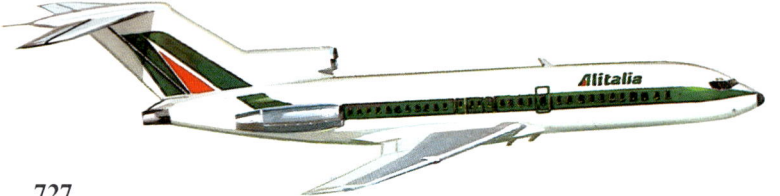

727

The Boeing 727 is one of the most successful airliners ever built. It is the only commercial transport aircraft of which more than 1500 examples have been sold. The three-engine arrange-ment was pioneered by the 727 and Trident, but the former proved far more successful.

Wing span: 32·98 m (108 ft. 0 in.)
Length: 40·59/46·69 m (133 ft. 2 in. or 153 ft. 2 in.)
Passengers: 94–189
Cruise speed: 872–953 km/h (542–592 mph)

737

The Boeing 737 is yet another success story for this manufac-turer. The series is being im-proved, with a stretched fusel-age, more economical engines, and refinements to the wing.

Wing span: 28·35 m (93 ft. 0 in.)
Length: 28·65–33·40 m (94 ft. 0 in. to 109 ft. 7 in.)
Passengers: 115–149
Cruise speed: 775–856 km/h (485–532 mph)

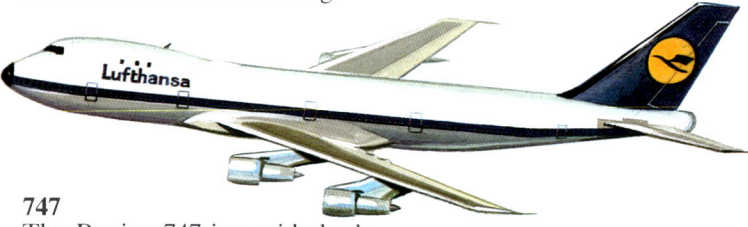

747

The Boeing 747 is a wide-body long-haul commercial trans-port, retaining the swept-wing, four underslung engine arrange-ment pioneered on the 707. The 747-300 has a stretched upper deck, providing accommoda-tion for 59 more passengers.

Wing span: 59·64 m (195 ft. 8 in.)
Length: 70·66 m (231 ft. 10 in.)
Passengers: 447–575
Max cruise speed: 980 km/h (609 mph)

747SP

The Boeing 747SP is a short-body version of the 747, designed to carry reduced payloads over extremely long routes. It is distinguished from the standard 747 by its short fuselage and taller fin.

Wing span: 59·64 m (195 ft. 8 in.)
Length: 56·31 m (184 ft. 9 in.)
Passengers: 331–440
Max cruise speed: 980 km/h (609 mph)

757

The Boeing 757 is the first of a new family of airliners, using the latest aerodynamics and turbofan technologies. Unlike the 767, the 757 retains the same fuselage cross section as the previous 707/727/737 generation. The narrow fuselage and two massive engines make recognition easy.

Wing span: 37·95 m (124 ft. 6 in.)
Length: 47·32 m (155 ft. 3 in.)
Passengers: 178–239
Cruise speed: 850–917 km/h (528–570 mph)

767

The Boeing 767 is a wide-body medium-haul commercial transport in broadly the same category as the Airbus A310. The Boeing aircraft places more emphasis on short field performance and long range. The two designs differ in such details as nose shape, and the precise form of wing, tail and engine pylons.

Wing span: 47·65 m (156 ft. 4 in.)
Length: 48·51/54·10 m (159 ft. 2 in. or 177 ft. 6 in.)
Passengers: 211–290
Cruise speed: 850–895 km/h (528–556 mph)

127

TriStar

The Lockheed L-1011 TriStar is a three-engined medium/long-haul wide-body transport aircraft. Unlike the earlier 727/Trident layouts, the L-1011 has two engines slung under the wings. Note that the centre-line engine is buried in the fuselage behind the cabin.

Wing span: 47·34/50·09 m (155 ft. 4 in. or 164 ft. 4 in.)
Length: 54·17/50·05 m (177 ft. 8½ in. or 164 ft. 2½ in.)
Passengers: 256–400
Cruise speed: 890–973 km/h (553–605 mph)

DC-8

The McDonnell Douglas DC-8 began life looking very like the 707, but could be distinguished by details such as the twin intakes under the nose. The Super 60 series was developed for very long ranges with varying degrees of cabin stretch. The Super 70 series is based on the 60, but has large turbofan engines (the CFM56).

Wing span: 43·41 or 45·23 m (142 ft. 5 in. or 148 ft. 5 in.)
Length: 45·87 to 57·12 m (150 ft. 6 in. to 187 ft. 5 in.)
Passengers: 179–259
Cruise speed: 854–965 km/h (531–600 mph)

DC-9

DC-9

The McDonnell Douglas DC-9 is one of the most successful short/medium haul airliners, rivalling the Boeing 737. It has gone through various stages of 'stretch', the longest in the basic DC-9 family being the Series 50.

Wing span: 28·47 m (93 ft. 5 in.)
Length: 36·37–40·72 m (119 ft. 3½ in. to 133 ft. 7¼ in.)
Passengers: 90–139
Cruise speed: 821–926 km/h (510–575 mph)

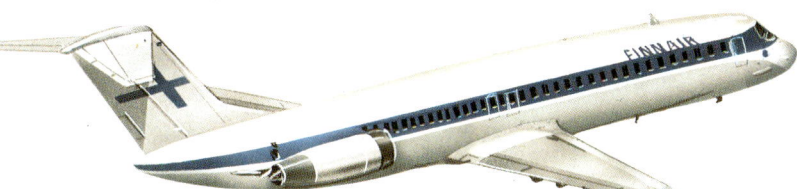

MD-80

The McDonnell Douglas MD-80 was originally known as the DC-9 Super 80. Based on the DC-9, it has a stretched fuselage, wingtip extensions, and highly economical turbofan engines. The elongated cabin and high aspect ratio wings are easily recognized.

Wing span: 32·87 m (107 ft. 10 in.)
Length: 45·06 m (147 ft. 10 in.)
Passengers: 155–172
Cruise speed: 840–924 km/h (522–574 mph)

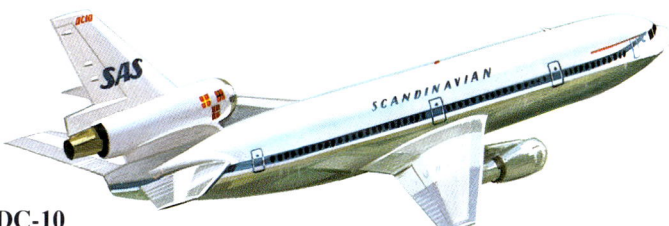

DC-10

The McDonnell Douglas DC-10 is a wide-body medium-haul commercial transport. Like the TriStar, it has three turbofan engines, but in this case the centre-line engine is mounted on the vertical tail, rather than buried in the rear fuselage. Some members of the DC-10 series have an additional two wheels on the centre-line, to permit higher weights.

Wing span: 47·34/50·41 m (155 ft. 4 in. or 165 ft. 4½ in.)
Length: 55·5 m (182 ft. 1 in.)
Passengers: 255–380
Cruise speed: 870–956 km/h (540–594 mph)

129

Airliners (20-99 seats)

EMB-120 Brasilia

The Embraer EMB-120 Brasilia is one of the new generation of commuter aircraft or regional transports, using two advanced turboprop engines. The low wing and T-tail configuration are good recognition points.

Wing span: 19·78 m (64 ft. 10¾ in.)
Length: 20 m (65 ft. 7½ in.)
Passengers: 24–30
Cruise speed: 467–533 km/h (290–331 mph)

Dash-7

The de Havilland Canada Dash-7 (DHC-7) is a STOL regional airliner powered by four turboprop engines. As a large aircraft that is sufficiently quiet to operate into city-centre airstrips, the Dash-7 is in a class of its own. In Canadian military service the designation CC-132 applies.

Wing span: 28·35 m (93 ft. 0 in.)
Length: 24·58 m (80 ft. 7¾ in.)
Passengers: 50–54
Cruise speed: 399–428 km/h (248–266 mph)

130

Dash-8

The de Havilland Canada Dash-8 (DHC-8) is a twin-turboprop regional transport in the new 30–40 seat class. It fits neatly between DHC's well-established 19-seat DHC-6 Twin Otter and the 50-seat Dash-7. Note the high wing and T-tail.

Wing span: 25.6 m (84 ft. 0 in.)
Length: 22·25 m (73 ft. 0 in.)
Passengers: 24–36
Max cruise speed: 500 km/h (312 mph)

CN-235

The Airtech CN-235 is a twin-turboprop regional airliner, jointly developed by CASA of Spain and Nurtanio of Indonesia. The high wing, upswept rear fuselage, and fuselage-mounted undercarriage make this design especially suitable for military variants. A stretched CN-235 seating up to 59 is also planned.

Wing span: 25·81 m (84 ft. 8 in.)
Length: 21·35 m (70 ft. 0¾ in.)
Passengers: 34–39
Max cruise speed: 454 km/h (282 mph)

ATR-42

The ATR-42 is a joint venture by France's Aérospatiale and Italy's Aeritalia. Its abbreviated name simply means 42-seat regional transport aircraft *(Avion de Transport Régional)*. Although the high-wing, T-tail arrangement is similar to that of the Dash-8, the ATR-42 is easily distinguished by its fuselage-mounted undercarriage and shorter nacelles (covering the engines). The rear fuselage is less upswept than that of the CN-235.

Wing span: 24·57 m (80 ft. 7½ in.)
Length: 22·67 m (74 ft. 4½ in.)
Passengers: 42–49
Max cruise speed: 510 km/h (317 mph)

SF-340

The Saab-Fairchild SF-340 is said to be the leader of the new 30–40 seat twin-turboprop regional airliners, having first flown in January 1983. Like the Brasilia, it has a low-set wing, but the SF-340 may be distinguished by its fuselage-mounted tailplane and shorter nose.

Wing span: 21·44 m (70 ft. 4 in.)
Length: 19·72 m (64 ft. 8 in.)
Passengers: 16–34
Cruise speed: 430–508 km/h (267–315 mph)

F27 Friendship

The Fokker F27 Friendship is the most successful airliner in its class, with over 750 sold (including 205 built by Fairchild in the US). The series includes the stretched Mk 500. The F27 is to be superseded by the 50-seat Fokker 50, which will be longer.

Wing span: 29.0 m (95 ft. 2 in.)
Length: 23·56/25·06 m (77 ft. 3½ in. or 82 ft. 2½ in.)
Passengers: 44–56
Typical cruise speed: 480 km/h (298 mph)

F28 Fellowship

The Fokker F28 Fellowship is a twin-turbofan short/medium haul transport, somewhat similar in general configuration to the DC-9, but much smaller. The airbrakes at the rear of the fuselage are an unusual feature. The F28 is to be joined by the 107-seat **Fokker 100**, which will be larger and have more efficient engines.

Wing span: 25·07 m (82 ft. 3 in.)
Length: 27·40/29·61 m (89 ft. 10¾ in. or 97 ft. 1¼ in.)
Passengers: 55–85
Cruise speed: 783–843 km/h (487–523 mph)

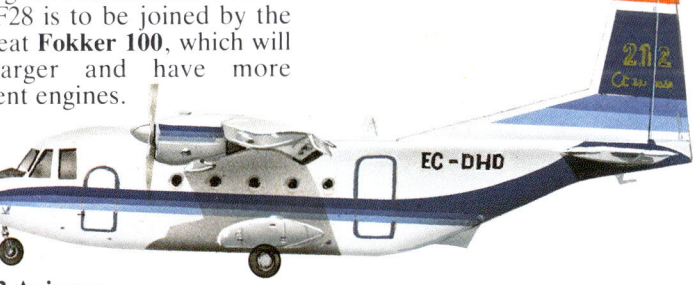

C-212 Aviocar

The CASA C-212 Aviocar is a small twin-turboprop transport for both civil and military applications. Note the square-section unpressurized fuselage, non-retractable undercarriage, and upswept rear end, with a loading ramp for vehicles.

Wing span: 19 m (62 ft. 4 in.)
Length: 15·16 m (49 ft. 9 in.)
Passengers: 24–28
Cruise speed: 346–365 km/h (215–227 mph)

Tu-134

The Tupolev Tu-134 is a twin-turbofan short/medium haul airliner. For its class, it has a relatively high degree of wing sweep. Note the characteristic wing trailing-edge fairings, housing the main landing gear wheels.

Wing span: 29·0 m (95 ft. 1¾ in.)
Length: 34·35 m (112 ft. 8¼ in.)
Passengers: 72
Max cruise speed: 870 km/h (540 mph)

BAe 748

The British Aerospace BAe 748 is a short/medium range twin-turboprop airliner, the principal rival of the Fokker F27. The 748 is to be superseded by the BAe ATP (Advanced Turboprop), which has a stretched cabin and new technology engines.

Wing span: 30·02/31·23 m (98 ft. 6 in. or 102 ft. 5½ in.)
Length: 20·42 m (67 ft. 0 in.)
Passengers: 40–58
Cruise speed: 452 km/h (281 mph)

BAe 146

The British Aerospace BAe 146 is a short-haul transport of unusual configuration, having four engines set under a high wing. Marketed as an F27 replacement, the BAe 146 is in direct competition with the F28 and Fokker 100. The main advantage of the BAe 146 appears to lie in the quietness of its high-bypass turbofans.

Wing span: 26·34 m (86 ft. 5 in.)
Length: 26·16/28·55 m (85 ft. 10 in./93 ft. 8 in.)
Passengers: 71–109
Cruise speed: 709–778 km/h (440–483 mph)

One-Eleven

The BAe One-Eleven is a twin-turbofan regional transport in broadly the same category as the DC-9, although the British aircraft has been far less successful. In 1979 BAe reached an agreement with CNIAR of Romania, under which the aircraft would be licence-built as the **Rombac 1-11**.

Wing span: 28·5 m (93 ft. 6 in.)
Length: 28·50/32·61 m (93 ft. 6 in. or 107 ft. 0 in.)
Passengers: 65–109
Cruise speed: 760–870 km/h (472–541 mph)

Shorts 360

The Shorts 360 is a long-body, single-fin derivative of the 330. The square-section fuselage provides far more headroom than is available in its pressurized (circular-section) rivals. The 360's high, braced wing, undercarriage pods, and single swept fin are unmistakable.

Wing span: 22·81 m (74 ft. 10 in.)
Length: 21·59 m (70 ft. 10 in.)
Passengers: 36
Max cruise speed: 393 km/h (244 mph)

Shorts 330

The Shorts 330 is a small twin-turboprop regional transport, easily distinguished by its square-section fuselage, high wing, bracing struts, main undercarriage fairings, and twin vertical tails. It is offered in several versions, including the Sherpa freighter, which forms the basis for the C-23A produced for the USAF.

Wing span: 22·76 m (74 ft. 8 in.)
Length: 17·69 m (58 ft. 0½ in.)
Passengers: 30
Cruise speed: 296–352 km/h (184–218 mph)

Commuter Aircraft

EMB-110 Bandeirante

The Embraer EMB-110 Bandeirante is a twin-turboprop light transport, named after the pioneers who opened up Brazil. Over 400 have been built for service in more than 20 countries. The Bandeirante is probably the most widely-used aircraft ever developed in the southern hemisphere.

Wing span: 15·33 m (50 ft. 3½ in.)
Length: 15·1 m (49 ft. 6½ in.)
Passengers: 18–21
Cruise speed: 335–413 km/h (208–257 mph)

Twin Otter

The de Havilland Canada Twin Otter is a highly successful twin-turboprop STOL transport with a fixed undercarriage and a strut bracing the high wing. More than 800 Twin Otters are operating in over 70 countries. The military version is designated CC-138 in Canadian service, and UV-18 in the US Army and USAF.

Wing span: 19·81 m (65 ft. 0 in.)
Length: 15·77 m (51 ft. 9 in.)
Passengers: 18–20
Max cruise speed: 338 km/h (210 mph)

L-410

The Let L-410 is a Czech-developed twin-turboprop general purpose transport air-craft. Well over 500 are in service, including many on Aeroflot's internal feederline services. The high wing, mid-set dihedral tailplane, and large sponsons for the main gear are distinctive features.

Wing span: 19·48 m (63 ft. 10¾ in.)
Length: 14·47 m (47 ft. 5½ in.)
Passengers: 15
Cruise speed: 300–365 km/h (186–227 mph)

Do 128

The Dornier Do 128 is the current production version of the Do 28D-2 Skyservant. It is built in two basic variants: the piston-engined Do 128-2, and the turboprop Do 128-6. In both cases the engines are mounted on low-set stub wings. The Do 128 has a fixed tailwheel under-carriage, the main units mounted below the engines.

Wing span: 15·55 m (51 ft. 0¼ in.)
Length: 11·41 m (37 ft. 5¼ in.)
Passengers: 8
Max cruise speed: 304/333 km/h (189/205 mph)

137

Do 228

The Dornier Do 228 retains the fuselage cross-section of the Do 128, but in other respects appears to be a completely new design. The engines (turboprops) are moved up to the wing, the stub wings deleted, and the main undercarriage units retract into fuselage fairings. The wing is of advanced design, with unusual triangular wingtips.

Wing span: 16·97 m (55 ft. 8 in.)
Length: 15·04/16·56 m (49 ft. 4 in. or 54 ft. 4 in.)
Passengers: 15/19
Cruise speed: 324–432 km/h (201–268 mph)

An-28

The Antonov AN-28 (NATO code-name Cash) is an enlarged, twin-turboprop derivative of the piston-engined An-14. The An-28 is being built in Poland by PZL Mielec. It is differentiated from the L-410 by its fixed undercarriage, twin vertical tails, and wing struts.

Wing span: 22·07 m (72 ft. 7 in.)
Length: 13·1 m (42 ft. 11¾ in.)
Passengers: 17–20
Cruise speed: 337 km/h (209 mph)

Jetstream

Jetstream

The British Aerospace Jetstream 31 is a twin turboprop business aircraft and regional airliner. Note the wide ('walk tall') cabin diameter.

Wing span: 15·85 m (52 ft. 0 in.)
Length: 14·37 m (47 ft. 1½ in.)
Passengers: 8–18
Cruise speed: 426–488 km/h (264–303 mph)

Islander

The Pilatus Britten-Norman BN-2B Islander is a small feederline transport, powered by two piston engines. Options include an extended nose for extra baggage, and extended tips. It is built in the UK, Romania, and the Philippines.

Wing span: 14·94/16·15 m (49 ft. 0 in. or 53 ft. 0 in.)
Length: 10·86/12·02 m (35 ft. 7¾ in. or 39 ft. 5¼ in.)
Passengers: 9
Cruise speed: 241–264 km/h (150–164 mph)

Trislander

The Pilatus Britten-Norman Trislander is a stretched derivative of the Islander, with a third engine mounted on the vertical tail. In late 1982 production was switched to the International Aviation Corp in Florida, where it is to be built under the name Tri-Commutair.

Wing span: 16·15 m (53 ft. 0 in.)
Length: 13·34 m (43 ft. 9 in.)
Passengers: 17
Cruise speed: 290 km/h (180 mph)

Beech C99

The Beech C99 Airliner is a twin-turboprop commuter transport, effectively a large derivative of the King Air B100 series of business transports. Note the fuselage-mounted tailplane and the square windows. Options include a belly-mounted baggage/cargo pod.

Wing span: 13·98 m (45 ft. 10½ in.)
Length: 13·58 m (44 ft. 6¾ in.)
Passengers: 15
Cruise speed: 454–461 km/h (282–287 mph)

Beech 1900

The Beech 1900 is a twin-turboprop commuter airliner, executive or cargo transport, derived from the Super King Air B200 series of executive transports. The rear-end design is unusual: a T-tail with small 'taillets' below the tailplane tips, and auxiliary horizontal surfaces ('stabilons') on the rear fuselage.

Wing span: 16·61 m (54 ft. 5¾ in.)
Length: 17·63 m (57 ft. 10 in.)
Passengers: 12–19
Max cruise speed: 442–487 km/h (275–302 mph)

Metro III

The Fairchild Metro III is one of the best-known twin turboprop commuter airliners. It is easily recognized by its long tubular fuselage and mid-set tailplane. The Metro IIIA is an advanced version with different engines, and the intakes below the propeller spinners.

Wing span: 17·37 m (57 ft. 0 in.)
Length: 18·09 m (59 ft. 4¼ in.)
Passengers: 19/20
Max cruise speed: 487–515 km/h
(303–320 mph)

Piper T-1020

The Piper T-1020 is a commuter version of the Piper Chieftain, with modified cabin, doors and undercarriage to suit high intensity operations. The T-1040 has the same fuselage, but turboprop engines in place of pistons, and the wings of the Cheyenne IIXL.

Wing span: 12·4 m (40 ft. 8 in.)
Length: 10·55 m (34 ft. 7½ in.)
Passengers: 9–10
Cruise speed: 315–372 km/h
(196–231 mph)

141

Business Jets

Challenger

The Canadair CL-600/601 Challenger is a twin turbofan business or commuter transport. It combines an extremely large cabin diameter with long range capability. The Challenger is built in two versions: the 'transcontinental' CL-600, and the 'intercontinental' CL-601, which has more efficient engines and winglets. In service with the Canadian Armed Forces, it is known as the CC-144.

Wing span: 18·85/19·61 m (61 ft. 10 in. or 64 ft. 4 in.)
Length: 20·85 m (68 ft. 5 in.)
Passengers: up to 19
Cruise speed: 745–833 km/h (463–518 mph)

Falcon 200

The Dassault-Breguet Mystère/Falcon 200 is the latest form of the twin-turbofan light business jet series produced by this French manufacturer, originally under the name Mystère 20. In the US this series is marketed as the Fan Jet Falcon. It exists in both civil and military forms, and represents the basis for the **HU-25A Guardian** sold to the US Coast Guard.

Wing span: 16·3 m (53 ft. 6 in.)
Length: 17·15 m (56 ft. 3 in.)
Passengers: 9–12
Cruise speed: 780–870 km/h (485–541 mph)

Falcon 50

The Dassault-Breguet Mystère/ Falcon 50 is a three-engined derivative of the 20/200 series, with a new wing design. An extremely long range is provided: in 1980 a Falcon 50 flew non-stop for a distance of 6159 km (3827 miles), and reached a height of 13,716 m (45,000 ft.), both class records.

Wing span: 18·86 m (61 ft. 10½ in.)
Length: 18·5 m (69 ft. 8½ in.)
Passengers: 8–12
Max cruise speed: 880 km/h (550 mph)

**Westwind 2
(improved version)**

Westwind I

The Israel Aircraft Industries IAI 1124 Westwind I is based on the American-built Jet Commander, but has turbofan engines in place of turbojets. The Westwind I is one of the few business jets with a straight wing. A maritime patrol version operated by the Israeli Navy is known as the **1124 Sea Scan**.

Wing span: 13·65 m (44 ft. 9½ in.)
Length: 15·93 m (52 ft. 3 in.)
Passengers: up to 10
Econ cruise speed: 741 km/h (460 mph)

Astra

The Israel Aircraft Industries IAI 1125 Astra is a swept-wing derivative of the Westwind series, with a slightly longer cabin and improved headroom, since the wing structure passes below (rather than through) the cabin. First flight took place on 19 March 1984.

Wing span: 16·05 m (52 ft. 8 in.)
Length: 16·94 m (55 ft. 7 in.)
Passengers: 6–9
Max cruise speed: 876 km/h (545 mph)

143

Diamond I

The Mitsubishi Diamond I/IA is a small twin-turbofan business jet with a swept wing. It can be distinguished from the Mystère/Falcon 100 series by its T-tail, its cockpit transparencies, and its six windows on either side of the cabin. Final assembly takes place in San Angelo, Texas.

Wing span: 13·25 m (43 ft. 6 in.)
Length: 14·75 m (48 ft. 5 in.)
Passengers: 7
Cruise speed: 741 km/h (461 mph)

BAe 125

The British Aerospace BAe 125 is a swept-wing, twin-turbofan business jet, in broadly the same category as the Mystère/Falcon 200 series. The British aircraft may be distinguished by its lower-set wing, smaller angle of sweep back, rather higher tailplane, and six cabin windows (rather than five). The BAe 125 is built in two versions: the 700 and 800 series, the latter having more powerful engines, increased length and span, a curved windscreen, and other refinements.

Wing Span: 14·33/15·66 m (47 ft. 0 in. or 51 ft. 4½ in.)
Length: 15·46/15·60 m (50 ft. 8½ in. or 51 ft. 2 in.)
Passengers: 8–14
Cruise speed: 723–858 km/h (449–533 mph)

Citation I

The Cessna Citation I is a small twin-turbofan business transport with a straight wing, providing the capability to operate from small airfields. The Citation II is a stretched version, taking up to 10 passengers, and with six cabin windows instead of four.

Wing Span: 14·35 m (47 ft. 1 in.)
Length: 13·26 m (43 ft. 6 in.)
Passengers: 5–7
Cruise speed: 662 km/h (411 mph)

Citation III

The Cessna Citation III is a twin-turbofan medium-size long range business transport. Although retaining the Citation name, it is a completely new design, with a swept wing. The Citation III established two time-to-height records for its class in 1983, and is claimed to be able to operate from shorter airfields than its competitors.

Wing Span: 16·31 m (53 ft. 6 in.)
Length: 16·9 m (55 ft. 5½ in.)
Passengers: up to 9
Max cruise speed: 874 km/h (543 mph)

Learjet 25D

The Gates Learjet 25D is a twin-turbojet light business transport, the basic model of the range. Despite its virtually unswept wing, the 25D has a high cruise speed, and is cleared to operate at 15,545 m (51,000 ft.).

Wing Span: 10·84 m (35 ft. 7 in.)
Length: 14·5 m (47 ft. 7 in.)
Passengers: up to 8
Cruise speed: 793–835 km/h
(493–519 mph)

Learjet 55

The Gates Learjet 55 is a twin-turbofan business transport. It represents the second major Learjet, with a wide-body cabin (in which it is now possible to stand up) and winglets. This model was originally to have been known as the 'Longhorn 55', because of the shape of the winglets.

Wing Span: 13·34 m (43 ft. 9 in.)
Length: 16·79 m (55 ft. 1 in.)
Passengers: 4–8
Cruise speed: 776–843 km/h
(482–524 mph)

Peregrine

Peregrine

The Gulfstream Aerospace Peregrine or Commander Fanjet 1500 is a small business transport with a single turbofan engine. It is derived from the company's Peregrine jet trainer. Note the inverted winglets and dorsal air intake.

Wing Span: 11·94 m (39 ft. 2 in.)
Length: 12·84 m (42 ft. 1½ in.)
Passengers: 6
Cruise speed: 542–613 km/h (337–381 mph)

Gulfstream III

The Gulfstream Aerospace Gulfstream III is a wide-body twin-turbofan business jet providing long range capability. It differs from the earlier 'G.II' in having a new wing with winglets, a more pointed nose, and extra fuel. However, some G.IIs are being converted to take the G.III wing, becoming the **G.IIB**. The **G.IV** is an improved version, distinguished by a sixth cabin window.

Wing Span: 23·72 m (77 ft. 10 in.)
Length: 25·32 m (83 ft. 1 in.)
Passengers: up to 19
Cruise speed: 818–928 km/h (508–576 mph)

Lear Fan

The Lear Fan 2100 is a twin turboprop light business transport, combining several advanced features. The straight wing and Vee-tail with underfin are unmistakable. Its engines are mounted on the side of the rear fuselage, and drive a single propeller in the tail. The Lear Fan is built almost entirely of advanced composite materials.

Wing Span: 11·99 m (39 ft. 4 in.)
Length: 12·37 m (40 ft. 7 in.)
Passengers: 7–9
Cruise speed: 519–673 km/h (322–418 mph)

Light Twin-engined Aircraft

EMB-121 Xingu

The Embraer EMB-121 Xingu is a good-looking twin-turbo-prop executive transport, used by both civil and military operators. The Xingu II has more powerful engines, and is recognized by its four-blade propellers and strakes on the rear fuselage.

Wing Span: 14·05 m (46 ft. 1¼ in.)
Length: 12·25 m (40 ft. 2¼ in.)
Passengers: 5–9
Cruise speed: 365–465 km/h (227–289 mph)

P.68C Victor

The Partenavia P.68C Victor is a twin-piston-engined high-wing light aircraft with a fixed tricycle undercarriage. Variants include two with retractable gears, and the glazed-nose **P.68 Observer**. A turboprop version jointly developed with Aeritalia was originally known as the P.68 Turbo, then the AP.68TP, and is now designated Spartacus.

Wing Span: 12 m (39 ft. 4½ in.)
Length: 9·55 m (31 ft. 4 in.)
Passengers: 6
Cruise speed: 272–318 km/h (169–198 mph)

P.166

The Piaggio P.166-DL3 is a twin-turboprop version of the earlier piston-engined P.166. The gull wing mounted high on the fuselage and the pusher engine installation are distinctive features.

Wing Span: 13·51 m (44 ft. 4 in.)
Length: 11·88 m (39 ft. 0 in.)
Passengers: 8
Cruise speed: 300–370 km/h (186–230 mph)

Marquise

The Mitsubishi Marquise is the current production designation for the high-wing, twin-turboprop executive transport previously sold as the MU-2N. The company also produces a short-body model, designated Solitaire (earlier MU-2P).

Wing Span: 11·94 m (39 ft. 2 in.)
Length: 12·02 m (39 ft. 5 in.)
Passengers: up to 10
Cruise speed: 547–571 km/h (340–355 mph)

PC-6

The Pilatus PC-6 Turbo-Porter is a STOL multi-role utility aircraft, powered by a single turboprop engine. It derives from the earlier PC-6 Porter, which had a piston engine. Well over 400 PC-6s of all models are in service in more than 50 countries.

Wing Span: 15·13 m (49 ft. 8 in.)
Length: 10·9 m (35 ft. 9 in.)
Passengers: up to 10
Cruise speed: 240–259 km/h (150–161 mph)

Duchesse 76

The Beech Duchesse 76 is a four-seat light aircraft powered by two piston engines. The T-tail, sharply upswept, untapered outer wings and flat engine nacelles are distinctive features.

Wing Span: 11·58 m (38 ft. 0 in.)
Length: 8·86 m (29 ft. 0½ in.)
Passengers: 3
Cruise speed: 280–308 km/h (174–191 mph)

Baron

The Beech Baron 58TC is a turbocharged version of the 4/6-seat twin-piston Baron light aircraft series. There are several products in the low-wing, light twin category, which are generally distinguished by the shape of the tail surfaces and the cabin transparencies.

Wing Span: 11·53 m (37 ft. 10 in.)
Length: 9·12 m (29 ft. 11 in.)
Passengers: up to 5
Cruise speed: 343–447 km/h (213–277 mph)

Duke

The Beech Duke B60 is a pressurized, 4/6-seat light aircraft powered by two turbocharged piston engines. Well over 500 Dukes have been produced. Note the dihedral tailplane and three cabin windows on each side.

Wing Span: 11·97 m (39 ft. 3¼ in.)
Length: 10·31 m (33 ft. 10 in.)
Passengers: up to 5
Cruise speed: 369–443 km/h (229–275 mph)

Super King Air

The Beech Super King Air 200 is a development of the preceding King Air 100, with a T-tail, more powerful engines, increased wing span, and various refinements. Note that the King Air F90 also has the T-tail, and is distinguished by the short cabin, with only three windows each side.

Wing Span: 16·61 m (54 ft. 6 in.)
Length: 13·34 m (43 ft. 9 in.)
Passengers: up to 14
Cruise speed: 523–536 km/h (325–333 mph)

151

Cessna 340

Wing Span: 11·62 m (38 ft. 1¼ in.)
Length: 10·46 m (34 ft. 4 in.)
Passengers: up to 5
Cruise speed: 315–425 km/h (196–264 mph)

The Cessna Model 340 is a 6-seat pressurized business aircraft, powered by two turbocharged piston engines. Whereas Cessna's single-engined aircraft have high wings, the light twins are low-winged. Note the small, oval cabin windows.

Cessna 421 Golden Eagle

Wing Span: 12·53 m (41 ft. 1½ in.)
Length: 11·09 m (36 ft. 4½ in.)
Passengers: up to 7
Cruise speed: 283–447 km/h (176–278 mph)

The Cessna Model 421 Golden Eagle represents the top of the company's twin-piston range. The Model 414 Chancellor is similar, but has a longer-span wing and less powerful engines.

Conquest II

The Cessna Conquest II is the top of Cessna's twin-turboprop range. It is distinguished from the Model 421, by the different nacelle shape and dihedral tail.

Wing Span: 15·04 m (49 ft. 4 in.)
Length: 11·89 m (39 ft. 0¼ in.)
Passengers: up to 10
Cruise speed: 456–543 km/h (283–337 mph)

Merlin

The Fairchild Merlin IIIC is the latest model of this handsome twin-turboprop executive transport. Note the large cabin windows, the engine air intakes over the spinners, and the medium-high tailplane. The **Merlin IVC** (despite its name) is a corporate version of the longer Metro III regional airliner.

Wing Span: 14·1 m (46 ft. 3 in.)
Length: 12·85 m (42 ft. 2 in.)
Passengers: up to 10
Max cruise speed: 556 km/h (345 mph)

Jetprop 1000

The Gulfstream Commander Jetprop 1000 is the latest of the series, differing from the **Jetprop 840** in having a longer cabin and more powerful engines.

Wing Span: 15·89 m (52 ft. 1½ in.)
Length: 13·1 m (42 ft. 11¾ in.)
Passengers: up to 11
Cruise speed: 474–571 km/h (295–355 mph)

153

PA-31-350 Chieftain

The Piper PA-31-350 Chieftain is a stretched version of the Navajo with more powerful engines. The extra cabin length is emphasized by the additional window on each side. Note that in the Piper designation system the final digits represent engine horsepower. The Chieftain is thus a Model 31 with 350 hp (piston) engines.

Wing Span: 12·4 m (40 ft. 8 in.)
Length: 10·55 m (34 ft. 7½ in.)
Passengers: up to 9
Cruise speed: 320–409 km/h (199–254 mph)

Cheyenne II

PA-42 Cheyenne III

The Piper PA-42 Cheyenne III is a twin-turboprop 6/11-seat business and commuter transport. It differs from the earlier **PA-31T Cheyenne I and II** in having a T-tail (rather than the tailplane mounted on the fuselage), a stretched cabin, increased wing span, and more powerful engines. The **Cheyenne IV** has turboprops of a different type, and can be recognized by the fact that there are no jetpipes at the front of the nacelles, and that the nacelles do not project beyond the wing trailing edge.

Wing Span: 14·53 m (47 ft. 8 in.)
Length: 12·23 m (43 ft. 4¾ in.)
Passengers: 6–10
Max cruise speed: 537 km/h (334 mph)

PA-31P-350 Mojave

The Piper PA-31P-350 Mojave combines a fuselage similar to that of the Cheyenne, the turbocharged piston engines of the Chieftain, and the wing of the Navajo. The 'P' in the Piper designation indicates that it is pressurized. The Mojave has three cabin windows on the right and two on the left.

Wing Span: 13·56 m (44 ft. 6 in.)
Length: 10·52 m (34 ft. 6 in.)
Passengers: 6
Cruise speed: 372–433 km/h (231–269 mph)

PA-60 Aerostar

The Piper PA-60 Aerostar 700P is a six-seat light transport, probably the world's fastest production twin-piston aircraft in its class. Note the unusual mid-wing setting. The Aerostar series has a very high standard of surface finish.

Wing Span: 11·18 m (36 ft. 8 in.)
Length: 10·61 m (34 ft. 9¾ in.)
Passengers: 5
Cruise speed: 448–471 km/h (279–292 mph)

Light Single-engined Aircraft

R.3140

The Avions Pierre Robin R.3140 is a low-cost all-metal four-seat light aircraft for touring and glider-tow duties. Note the T-tail and spatted tricycle undercarriage. Later members of the R.3000 series have more powerful engines, and a retractable undercarriage has been proposed.

Wing Span: 9·81 m (32 ft. 2¼ in.)
Length: 7·51 m (24 ft. 7¾ in.)
Passengers: 3
Cruise speed: 234–246 km/h (145–153 mph)

EA7 Optica

The Edgley EA7 Optica is a three-seat observation aircraft, which is claimed to be able to perform many of the roles of a helicopter (pipeline and forestry patrol, aerial photography, and TV reporting and so on) at only a fraction of the cost. It has three unusual features: the glazed cabin, the ducted fan powerplant, and the twin booms with connecting tailplane.

Wing Span: 11·99 m (39 ft. 4 in.)
Length: 8·15 m (26 ft. 9 in.)
Passengers: 2
Cruise speed: 174 km/h (108 mph)

Bonanza

The Beech Bonanza Model V35B is the latest form of one of the best known of general aviation aircraft, the V-tail Bonanza, which first flew in 1945. The Bonanza is also sold with a conventional tail arrangement, well over 15,000 of all models having been built.

Wing Span: 10·21 m (33 ft. 6 in.)
Length: 8·05 m (26 ft. 5 in.)
Passengers: 3/4
Cruise speed: 291–311 km/h (181–198 mph)

Lightning

The Beech Lightning Model 38P is a four/six seat light aircraft, one of the first general aviation products to be powered by a single turboprop. It is based on the airframe of the pressurized, twin-engined Baron 58P, and is offered with three different types of turboprop.

Wing Span: 11·58 m (38 ft. 0 in.)
Length: 9·14 m (30 ft. 0 in.)
Passengers: 3/5
Cruise speed: 383–520 km/h (238–323 mph)

157

Cessna 152

The Cessna 152 is the replacement for the old Model 150, introducing (from 1977) a more powerful engine, a better propeller, and many refinements. It has a fixed tricycle undercarriage, with optional spats. The Model 152 **Aerobat** has a stronger structure to allow certain aerobatics to be performed.

Wing Span: 9·97 m (32 ft. 8½ in.)
Length: 7·34 m (24 ft. 1 in.)
Passengers: 1
Max cruise speed: 196 km/h (122 mph)

Stationaire

The Cessna Stationaire is produced in both six and eight-seat models (the length quoted below refers to the stretched Stationaire 8). It has double cargo doors on the right side of the fuselage. The Stationaire represents the top of the fixed-gear, single-piston Cessna range.

Wing Span: 10·92 m (35 ft. 10 in.)
Length: 9·8 m (32 ft. 2 in.)
Passengers: 5/7
Max cruise speed: 298 km/h (185 mph)

Mooney 201

Mooney 201

The Mooney 201 is a four-seat light aircraft with a single piston engine. By tradition, Mooney designs have forward-swept fins and a designation that indicates the aircraft's maximum speed in mph.

Wing Span: 11 m (36 ft. 1 in.)
Length: 7·52 m (24 ft. 8 in.)
Passengers: 3
Cruise speed: 269–314 km/h
  (167–195 mph)

PA-28-161 Warrior

Aside from the venerable PA-18 Super Cub (now made by WTA in Texas) and the discontinued PA-38 Tomahawk, the PA-28-161 Warrior II represents the lower end of the Piper line. The PA-28 (previously refer-red to as the Cherokee line) also includes the PA-128-181 **Archer II**, the PA-28RT-201T **Turbo Arrow IV**, and the PA-128-236 **Dakota**.

Wing Span: 10·67 m (35 ft. 0 in.)
Length: 7·25 m (23 ft. 9½ in.)
Passengers: 3
Cruise speed: 191–235 km/h
  (119–146 mph)

PA-38-122 Tomahawk

The Piper PA-38-112 Toma-hawk was launched as a brand-new trainer and two-seat utility aircraft in 1978. Distinctive features included a wide-track fixed tricycle gear and a T-tail. Approximately 2500 had been built when production was en-ded in 1983, due to the effects of the general recession.

Wing Span: 10·36 m (34 ft. 0 in.)
Length: 7·04 m (23 ft. 1¼ in.)
Passengers: 1
Cruise speed: 185–200 km/h
  (115–124 mph)

159

PA-46-310P Malibu

The Piper PA-46-310P Malibu is a pressurized six-seat cabin monoplane, powered by a single turbocharged piston engine. It might be regarded as a high performance and more spacious replacement for the older **PA-32R-301T Turbo Saratoga SP**.

Wing Span: 13·11 m (43 ft. 0 in.)
Length: 8·66 m (28 ft. 4¾ in.)
Passengers: 5
Cruise speed: 365–400 km/h (226–248 mph)

Pitts Special

The Pitts Special S-2A is a two-seat version of the single-seat S-1 aerobatic biplane. Probably the best-known aircraft in its class, the S-1 first flew in 1944 and has won many contests. The Pitts Special is powered by a single piston engine, and some models are available for home construction.

Wing Span: 6·1 m (20 ft. 0 in.)
Length: 5·41 m (17 ft. 9 in.)
Passengers: 1
Max cruise speed: 245 km/h (152 mph)

Agricultural Aircraft

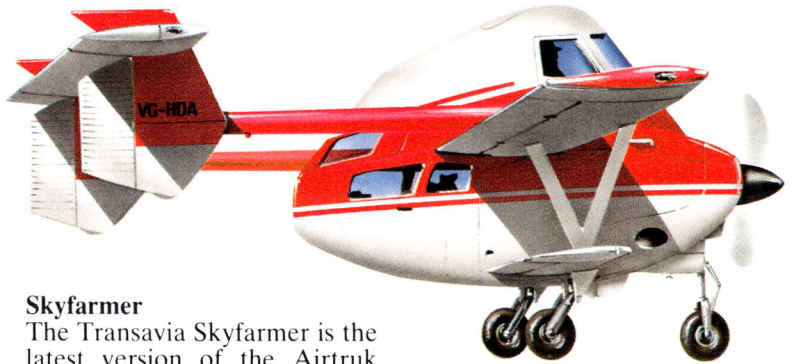

Skyfarmer

The Transavia Skyfarmer is the latest version of the Airtruk series, an unusual Australian agricultural aircraft of which well over 100 have been built. The deep central pod and twin tail booms are easy clues to its identity. The widely-spaced tails allow loading vehicles to drive close to the hopper.

Wing Span: 11·98 m (39 ft. 3½ in.)
Length: 6·35 m (20 ft. 10 in.)
Passengers: up to 5
Max cruise speed: 188 km/h (117 mph)

Cresco

New Zealand's Pacific Aerospace Corporation has developed the Cresco as a turboprop derivative of the **Fletcher FU24** piston-engined agricultural aircraft. Rights to the US-designed FU24 were bought by Air Parts (NZ) in 1964, and approximately 300 have been built, the company later being reformed as PAC. Note the upswept wingtips.

Wing Span: 12·81 m (42 ft. 0 in.)
Length: 11·06 m (36 ft. 3¼ in.)
Passengers: 1
Max cruise speed: 250 km/h (155 mph)

PZL-104 Wilga

Poland's PZL-104 Wilga (Thrush) is a general purpose four-seater with a single radial engine and a fixed tricycle undercarriage. Over 700 *Wilgas* have been built, mainly for agricultural and glider-tug roles. Note the pod-and-boom fuselage design and the full-span fixed leading edge slat.

Wing Span: 11·12 m (36 ft. 5¾ in.)
Length: 8·1 m (26 ft. 6¾ in.)
Passengers: up to 3
Cruise speed: 142–157 km/h (88–97 mph)

PZL 106 AT

PZL-106 Kruk

The PZL-106 Kruk (Raven) is a low-wing agricultural aircraft, powered by a radial engine. For identification, note the strut bracing for the slightly aft-swept wing, the swept-back fin, and the straight line from the top of the canopy to the base of the fin. A turboprop version has flown.

Wing Span: 14·80 m (48 ft. 6½ in.)
Length: 9·1 m (29 ft. 10½ in.)
Passengers: 1
Max cruise speed: 180 km/h (112 mph)

162

M-18 Dromader

The PZL M-18A Dromader (Dromedary) is a large agricultural aircraft, powered by a powerful radial engine, as fitted to the Antonov An-2 biplane. A much heavier aircraft than the PZL-106, it may be recognized by its unswept wing and tail surfaces, and the way in which the cockpit lines fall away to the slender rear fuselage.

Wing Span: 17·7 m (58 ft. 0¾ in.)
Length: 9·47 m (31 ft. 1 in.)
Passengers: nil
Cruise speed: 190–205 km/h
  (118–127 mph)

Ag Truck

The Cessna Ag Truck represents a break from the company's single-engined series in having a low wing. It is distinguished from the somewhat similar **Piper PA-36 Brave** by its strut-braced wing with downturned tips, and unswept vertical tail. The PA-36 is now built by WTA Inc. in Texas as the **New Brave.**

Wing Span: 12·7 m (41 ft. 8 in.)
Length: 7.90 m (25 ft. 11 in.)
Passengers: nil
Max cruise speed: 187 km/h (116 mph)

163

Ag-Cat

Rights to the Gulfstream American Ag-Cat are now owned by Schweizer Aircraft of New York. The company produces various models with radial and turboprop engines. This agricultural biplane is easily recognized, whether in its original uncowled piston-engined form, or with the long pointed nose of the **Ag-Cat Turbine**.

Wing Span: 12·93 m (42 ft. 5 in.)
Length: 7·47 m (24 ft. 6 in.)
Passengers: nil
Operating speed: 185 km/h (115 mph)

Sailplanes and Water Bombers

SF-34

The Scheibe Flugzeugbau SF-34 Delphin (Dolphin) is a tandem two-seat training and sporting sailplane. The company is also producing the **SF-36**, a motor glider using the wing and tail surfaces of the -34, but with side-by-side seating and a fixed tailwheel undercarriage.

Wing Span: 15·8 m (51 ft. 10 in.)
Length: 7.5 m (24 ft. 7¼ in.)
Seats: 2
Max glide ratio: 35/1

CL-215

The Canadair CL-215 is an amphibian powered by two radial engines, and normally employed as a water-bomber in fighting forest fires. However, it is also used for coastal patrol and as a passenger transport. In the fire-fighting role it can scoop water from the sea or a lake, while skimming over the surface at 130 km/h (81 mph). It takes about 10 seconds to scoop up the full load of 5246 litres (1176 Imp. gal.).

Wing Span: 28·6 m (93 ft. 10 in.)
Length: 19·82 m (65 ft. 0½ in.)
Passengers: 1–27 (depending on role)
Cruise speed: 291 km/h (181 mph)

G.109

The Grob G.109 is a two-seat motor-glider with a small piston engine in the nose. It is largely constructed of glassfibre, and has a fixed tailwheel undercarriage. Note the high aspect ratio of the wing, the slender rear fuselage, and the T-tail. Grob-Werke is a leading German sailplane manufacturer.

Wing Span: 16·6 m (54 ft. 5½ in.)
Length: 7·8 m (25 ft. 7 in.)
Seats: 2
Max glide ratio: 30/1

Civil Helicopters

AS.332 Super Puma

The Aérospatiale AS.332 Super Puma is a derivative of the earlier **SA.330 Puma**, with more powerful engines and many refinements. It may be distinguished by its longer nose, single mainwheels, and fin below the rear of the tailboom. The Super Puma is built in civil, military and naval versions, with several lengths of cabin.

Main rotor diameter: 15·6 m (51 ft. 2¼ in.)
Fuselage length: 14·76–16·25 m (48 ft. 5 in. to 53 ft. 3¾ in.)
Passengers: 8–21
Cruise speed: 260–280 km/h (161–173 mph)

AS.350 Ecureuil

The Aérospatiale AS.350 Ecureuil (Squirrel) is a light general-purpose helicopter, developed to replace the Alouette. A version with an American engine is assembled and marketed in the US under the name **AStar**. The **AS.355 Ecureuil 2** or **TwinStar** is a twin-engined version.

Main rotor diameter: 10·69 m (35 ft. 0¾ in.)
Fuselage length: 10·91 m (35 ft. 9½ in.)
Passengers: up to 5
Max cruise speed: 232 km/h (144 mph)

166

SA.365 Dauphin

The Aérospatiale SA.365 Dauphin 2 is a twin-engined derivative of the **SA.360 Dauphin**. It is produced in civil, military and naval versions, and the **SA.365N** is a variant of largely composite construction. The **SA.366** is a special model for the US Coast Guard, designated **HH-65A Dolphin**.

Main rotor diameter: 13·46 m (44 ft. 2 in.)
Fuselage length: 11·44 or 12·11 m (37 ft. 6½ in. or 39 ft. 8¾ in.)
Passengers: up to 13
Max cruise speed: 280 km/h (184 mph)

BO 105

The MBB BO 105 is a light utility helicopter, and one of West Germany's most succesful postwar aerospace products. It is powered by two turbine engines. The BO 105 is built in civil and military versions, including the **Twin Jet II** for the US corporate market, and an anti-tank model for the German Army (**BO 105P**).

Main rotor diameter: 9·84 m (32 ft. 3½ in.)
Fuselage length: 8·56 m (28 ft. 1 in.)
Passengers: up to 4
Cruise speed: 204–242 km/h (127–150 mph)

BK 117

The MBB/Kawasaki BK 117 is a joint development, aimed at producing a multi-purpose helicopter, benefiting from experience on the smaller BO 105. The production of components is split roughly equally between the two companies, each of which has a final assembly line.

Main rotor diameter: 11 m (36 ft. 1 in.)
Fuselage length: 9·98 m (32 ft. 9 in.)
Passengers: up to 10
Cruise speed: 230–251 km/h (143–156 mph)

A 109A

The **Agusta A 109A** is an eight-seat light utility helicopter with two turbine engines. Note the retractable undercarriage, up-swept rear fuselage, and distinctive underfin. It is built in several versions, including an ambulance model with 'bubble' doors to allow stretchers to be loaded across the fuselage. A military version was used by Argentina in the Falklands conflict.

Main rotor diameter: 11 m (36 ft. 1 in.)
Fuselage length: 10·71 m (35 ft. 1½ in.)
Passengers: up to 7
Cruise speed: 230–280 km/h (143–174 mph)

Ka-26 Hoodlum

The Kamov Ka-26 (NATO code-name **Hoodlum**) is mainly used for agricultural purposes, although it is also employed as an air ambulance, passenger transport, and general utility helicopter. It has the characteristic contra-rotating rotors ·of the Kamov series.

Rotor diameter: 13·0 m (42 ft. 8 in.)
Fuselage length: 7·75 m (25 ft. 5 in.)
Passengers: up to 7
Cruise speed: 90–150 km/h (56–93 mph)

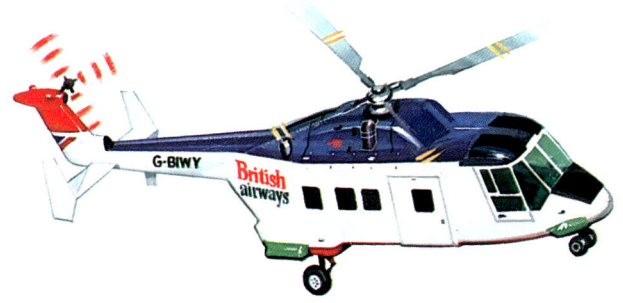

Westland 30

The Westland 30 is an enlarged derivative of the Lynx, with a high-capacity cabin allowing it to be used as a passenger/troop transport. It exists in several different versions, using either British or US engines. The fuselage shape and non-retracting undercarriage make it easy to identify.

Main rotor diameter: 13·31 m (43 ft. 8 in.)
Fuselage length: 14·33 m (47 ft. 0 in.)
Passengers: up to 19
Max cruise speed: 222 km/h (138 mph)

169

LongRanger

The Bell Model 206L LongRanger is a stretched and more powerful derivative of the Model 206 **JetRanger**. It has a single turbine engine, and the traditional Bell two-blade rotor, which produces a distinctive noise. The LongRanger is distinguished by its extra cabin windows. A military version is called the **TexasRanger**.

Main rotor diameter: 11·28 m (37 ft. 0 in.)
Fuselage length: 10·13 m (33 ft. 3 in.)
Passengers: up to 6
Max cruise speed: 203 km/h (126 mph)

TwinRanger

The Bell Model 400 TwinRanger is a new twin-engined derivative of the single-engined JetRanger/LongRanger series. Although largely a new design, the rotor is like that fitted to the military Model 406 (OH-58D). The 'Ring-Fin' tail rotor is an unusual feature.

Main rotor diameter: 10·67 m (35 ft. 0 in.)
Fuselage length: 10·31 m (33 ft. 10 in.)
Passengers: up to 6
Cruise speed: 259 km/h (161 mph)

Bell 222 UT

Bell 222

The Bell 222 is a twin-turbine engined light commercial helicopter. Recognition features include its retractable undercarriage with sponsons for the mainwheels, and its two-blade rotor. The basic model is the **222A**, the **222B** being an improved version with an increased rotor diameter and longer tailboom, making it more stable. The **222UT** (Utility Twin) is a variation of the 222B with skids.

Main rotor diameter: 12·12/12·80 m (39 ft. 9 in. or 42 ft. 0 in.)
Fuselage length: 12·50/12·85 m (41 ft. 0 in. or 42 ft. 2 in.)
Passengers: 7/9
Cruise speed: 246/259 km/h (153/161 mph)

Enstrom 280C Shark

The Enstrom Model F-280C Shark is a three-seat light helicopter, powered by a single turbocharged piston engine driving a three-blade main rotor. The Enstrom series has a distinctive fuselage shape and a tall rotor mast.

Main rotor diameter: 9·75 m (32 ft. 0 in.)
Length: 8·94 m (29 ft. 4 in.)
Passengers: 2
Cruise speed: 137–188 km/h (85–117 mph)

171

Hughes 300C

The Hughes 300C is a piston-engined light helicopter with a three-blade main rotor. Its cabin shape and slender tail-boom are good recognition features. The **300CQ** has special modifications to reduce noise, and the **Sky Night** is a version for police forces. Over 2750 built, including the **TH-55A** for the US Army. The series is now built only by Schweizer in the US and Bredanardi in Italy.

Main rotor diameter: 8·18 m (26 ft. 10 in.)
Length: 9·4 m (30 ft. 10 in.)
Passengers: 2
Cruise speed: 124–153 km/h (77–95 mph)

Hughes 500E

The Hughes 500E is a refined version of the Model 500 light utility helicopter, retaining the single turbine engine and four-blade rotor, but with a lengthened nose to increase leg-room for the front seats. The **530E** has the longer nose, but a more powerful engine to improve performance under hot or high conditions.

Main rotor diameter: 8·05 m (26 ft. 5 in.)
Fuselage length: 7·07 m (23 ft. 2½ in.)
Passengers: 4
Cruise speed: 233–258 km/h (145–160 mph)

Robinson R22

The Robinson R22 is a light-weight two-seat helicopter, originally developed to compete in price with corresponding two-seat fixed-wing aircraft. It has a single piston engine driving a two-blade main rotor. Its fuselage proportions are quite different from those of the Hughes 300 series.

Main rotor diameter: 7·67 m (25 ft. 2 in.)
Fuselage length: 6·3 m (20 ft. 8 in.)
Passengers: 1
Cruise speed: 153–177 km/h (95–110 mph)

S-76

The Sikorsky S-76 is a twin-turbine engined commercial transport helicopter with a retractable tricycle undercarriage. The main rotor is a scaled-down version of that on the military UH-60A. Though looking rather like a large Agusta A 109, the S-76 lacks the underfin of the Italian aircraft, and has a different nacelle shape.

Main rotor diameter: 13·41 m (44 ft. 0 in.)
Length: 16 m (52 ft. 6 in.)
Passengers: up to 12
Cruise speed: 232–286 km/h (144–178 mph)

173

Record Breakers

WORLD RECORDS: BALLOONS

DURATION:
137 hr 5 min 50 sec.
Aircraft: gas balloon Double
  Eagle II
Crew: M. L. Anderson, B. L.
  Abruzzo, and L. M. Newman
Date: 12–17 August 1978

ALTITUDE:
34,668 metres (113,740 ft.)
Aircraft: gas balloon
Crew: Cdr. M. D. Ross and Lt.
  Cdr. V. A. Prother
Date: 4 May 1961

DISTANCE:
8382.54 km (5208.67 miles)
Aircraft: gas balloon Double
  Eagle V
Crew: B. L. Abruzzo, L. M.
  Newman, R. Aoki, and R.
  Clark
Date: 9–12 November 1981
Location: Nagashima, Japan to
  Covello, California

WORLD RECORDS: HELICOPTERS

DISTANCE IN A STRAIGHT
LINE:
3561.55 km (2213 miles)
Aircraft: Hughes OH-6A
Pilot: R. G. Ferry
Date: 6–7 April 1966

ALTITUDE:
12,442 metres (40,820 ft.)
Aircraft: Aerospatiale SA 315B
  Lama
Pilot: J. Boulet
Date: 21 June 1972

SPEED IN A STRAIGHT
LINE:
368.4 km/h (222.9 mph)
Aircraft: Mil A-10 (Mi-24)
Pilot: G. Karapetyan
Date: 21 September 1978
Location: near Moscow

WORLD RECORDS: SAILPLANES

HEIGHT:
14,102 metres (42,266 ft.)
Aircraft: Schweizer SGS 1-23E
Pilot: Paul F. Bickle
Date: 25 February 1961
Location: Mojave, California

DISTANCE IN A STRAIGHT
LINE:
1460.8 km (907.7 miles)
Aircraft: Schleicher ASW 12
Pilot: Hans D. Grosse
Date: 25 April 1972

WORLD RECORDS: PISTON-ENGINED AEROPLANES

ALTITUDE:
17,083 metres (56,046 ft.)
Aircraft: Caproni Ca 161 bis
Pilot: Mario Pezzi
Date: 22 October 1938
Location: Italy

SPEED IN A STRAIGHT
LINE:
832.12 km/h (517.06 mph)
Aircraft: modified North
American P-51D Mustang
Pilot: Frank Taylor
Date: 30 July 1983
Location: Mojave, California

DISTANCE IN A STRAIGHT
LINE:
18,081.99 km (11,235.6 miles)
Aircraft: Lockheed P2V-1
Neptune
Pilot: Cdr. Thomas D. Davies,
USN
Date: 29 September–1 October
1946
Location: Perth, Australia to
Columbus, Ohio, USA

ABSOLUTE WORLD RECORDS: AEROPLANES

DISTANCE IN A STRAIGHT
LINE:
20,168.78 km (12,523.3 miles)
Aircraft: Boeing B-52H
Pilot: Major Clyde P. Evely,
USAF
Date: 10–11 January 1962
Location: Okinawa to Madrid

ALTITUDE:
37,650 metres (123,523 ft.) –
reached transiently in zoom.
Aircraft: E-266M (MiG–25)
Pilot: Alexander Fedotov
Date: 31 August 1977
Location: Soviet Union

SUSTAINED ALTITUDE:
25,929.031 metres (85,069 ft.)
Aircraft: Lockheed SR-71A
Crew: Capt. R. C. Helt and
Maj. L. A. Elliott, USAF
Date: 28 July 1976
Location: Beale AFB, California

ALTITUDE FROM AIR
LAUNCH
95,935.99 metres (314,750 ft.)
Aircraft: North American
X-15A
Pilot: Maj. R. White, USAF
Date: 17 July 1962
Location: Edwards AFB,
California

SPEED IN A STRAIGHT
LINE:
3529.56 km/h (2193.17 mph)
Aircraft: Lockheed SR-71A
Crew: Capt. E. W. Joersz and
Maj. G. T. Morgan, USAF
Date: 28 July 1976
Location: Beale AFB, California

Museums in Europe and the USA

BELGIUM
Musée de l'Air et de l'Espace (Brussels)

FRANCE
Jean Salis Collection (La Ferte Allais, near Paris)
Musée de l'Air (Le Bourget, Paris)

GERMANY
Deutsches Museum (Munich)
Hubschrauber Museum (Bückeburg)
Luftwaffe Museum (Uetersen)

ITALY
Museo Storico dell'Aeronautica Militare (Vigna de Valle)

NETHERLANDS
Aviadome (Schiphol, Amsterdam)

SWITZERLAND
Verkehrshaus (Lucerne)

UNITED KINGDOM
Cosford Aerospace Museum (Cosford, Shropshire)
Imperial War Museum (Lambeth, London and Duxford,
    Cambridgeshire)
Historic Aircraft Museum (St Athan, South Glamorgan)
Manchester Air and Space Museum
Midland Air Museum (Bagington, Coventry, Warwickshire)
Museum of Army Flying (Middle Wallop, Hampshire)
RAF Museum (Hendon, London)
Science Museum (South Kensington, London)
Shuttleworth Collection (Old Warden, Bedfordshire)

UNITED STATES
Air Museum (Chino, California)
Champlin Fighter Museum (Mesa, Arizona)
Confederate Air Force Museum (Harlingen, Texas)
National Air and Space Museum, Smithsonian Institution
    (Washington DC)
Naval Aviation Museum (Naval Air Station, Pensacola, Florida)
Pima Air Museum (Tucson, Arizona)
San Diego Aero-Space Museum (San Diego, California)
United States Air Force Museum (Wright-Patterson AFB,
    Drayton, Ohio)

Societies

There are a number of societies for aviation enthusiasts in the United Kingdom. Some of them produce their own journals and important works of reference. A few of them are listed here.

Air Britain (19 The Pastures, Westwood, Bradford-on-Avon, Wiltshire)
British Aviation Research Group (Paul Hewins, 8 Nightingale Road, Woodley, Berkshire RG5 3LP)

LAAS International (M. T. Reynolds, 37 Crane Close, Dagenham, Essex RM10 8LP)
Merseyside Aviation Society (Room 14, Hangar No. 2, Liverpool Airport, Merseyside L24 8QE)
Midland Counties Publications (24 The Hollow, Earl Shilton, Leicestershire LE9 7NA)
West London Aviation Group (Bob Parnell, 18 Green Lawns, Southbourne Gardens, Eastcote, Ruislip, Middlesex HA3 9SP)

Books to Read

There are a great many magazines specializing in aircraft. Ask your local newsagent about these. You will find books on aircraft in your local library or bookshop. The following reference books contain useful information and are particularly recommended:
Civil Aircraft Markings by A. Wright (Ian Allen, annually).
Jane's All the World's Aircraft edited by John W. R. Taylor (Jane's, annually).
Jane's World Aircraft Recognition Handbook by Derek Wood (Jane's, second edition 1985).
Militair 82 by John Andrade (Aviation Press, 1982).
Military Aviation Markings by P. March (Ian Allen, annually).
The Flier's Handbook edited by Varley (Pan Books, 1978).
The Observer's Book of Airliners by Green and Swanborough (Warne, annually).
The Observer's Directory of Military Aircraft (Warne, annually).

Airports and Airfields

The most interesting way to see aircraft is to visit the major airshows. Some airports also provide facilities for spectators. Readers in the United Kingdom may find it worthwhile to visit some of the following: **Abbotsinch** (Glasgow), **Aldergrove** (Belfast), **Castle Donnington** (East Midlands), **Dyce** (Aberdeen), **Gatwick, Heathrow, Luton, Ringway** (Manchester) and **Turnhouse** (Edinburgh).

The following military airfields may provide reasonable viewing and variety: **Manston** in Kent, **Mildenhall** in Suffolk, **St Mawgan** in Cornwall, **Valley** in North Wales and **Yeovilton** in Somerset.

Aircraft Abbreviations

AAA anti-aircraft artillery (flak)
AAC (British) Army Air Corps
AAC Australian Aircraft Consortium
AAM air-to-air missile
A/C aircraft
ACM air combat manoeuvre
ACT air combat training
ADC (USAF) Aerospace Defense Command
ADC air data computer
ADF automatic direction finding (also referred to as radio compass)
AEW airborne early warning (radar)
AFB (USAF) Air Force Base
AFCS automatic flight control system
AI air interception (radar)
ANG (USAF) Air National Guard
AOA angle of attack
APS aircraft prepared for service
APU auxiliary power unit
ARM anti-radar missile
ASI air speed indicator
ASM air-to-surface missile
ASV air-to-surface vessel (radar)
ASV anti-surface vessel (missile)
ASW anti-submarine warfare
ATC air traffic control
ATC (British) Air Training Corps
AUW all-up weight
AVGAS aviation gasoline (ie fuel for aircraft piston engines)
AVTUR aviation turbine (fuel)
AWACS Airborne Warning And Control System
BA British Airways
BAe British Aerospace
BCAR British Civil Airworthiness Requirements
BITE built-in test equipment
BVR beyond visual range (ref. engagements or missiles)
CAA (British) Civil Aviation Administration
CAB (US) Civil Aeronautics Board
CBU cluster bomb unit
CCV control-configured vehicle
CEP circle of equal probability (the radius of a circle containing half the bomb/bullet/missile strikes, thus giving a measure of accuracy)
CFRP carbonfibre-reinforced plastics

CG centre of gravity
c/n construction number
DACT dissimilar air combat training (ie, with different aircraft types)
daN decaNewton (a measure of force, roughly equal to 2·25 lb)
DARPA (US) Defense Advanced Research Projects Agency
dB decibel
DF direction finding
DME distance measuring equipment (navaid)
EAA (US) Experimental Aircraft Association
ECM electronic countermeasures (usually jamming)
elint electronic intelligence (ie the gathering and interpretation of information from enemy radio/radar transmissions)
ESM electronic support measures (usually in the form of a radar warning receiver)
EW electronic warfare
FAA (US) Federal Aviation Administration
FAC forward air control/controller (ie, the control of aircraft providing close air support for friendly troops)
FAI Fédération Aéronautique Internationale (the body responsible for supervising record attempts)
FAR (US) Federal Aviation Regulations
FBW fly-by-wire (ie, electrically-signalled controls)
FEBA forward edge of the battle area
FLIR forward-looking infra-red (sensors)
FSD full-scale development
FY (US) fiscal year
g acceleration due to gravity (thus, a fighter turning at 9*g* is producing a lift equal to nine times its weight)
GCI ground-controlled interception
GD General Dynamics
GE General Electric
GPU ground power unit
GPWS ground proximity warning system
GSE ground support equipment
GTS gas turbine starter
GW guided weapon
HF high frequency (radio)

HMS helmet-mounted sight
HP high pressure
hp horsepower
HUD head-up display
IAS indicated airspeed
IATA International Air Transport Association
ICAO International Civil Aviation Organisation
ICBMs intercontinental ballistic missile
IFF identification, friend or foe
IFR instrument flight rules
IGE in ground effect (ref. helicopter performance)
ILS instrument landing system
IMC instrument meteorological conditions
INS inertial navigation system
IOC initial operational capability
IP initial point (a navigation reference point in ground attack)
IRLS infra-red linescan
ISA International Standard Atmosphere
JASDF Japan Air Self-Defence Force
JATO jet-assisted take-off
JMSDF Japan Maritime Self-Defence Force
kg kilogram
km kilometre
kW kilowatt (equal to 1·34 hp)
LLTV low-light television
LP low pressure
M Mach (number)
MAC (USAF) Military Airlift Command
MAD magnetic anomaly detector (a device for finding submerged submarines)
MDC McDonnell Douglas Corporation
MMS mast-mounted sight (a helicopter sight mounted on top of the rotor)
MoD (British) Ministry of Defence
mph miles per hour
MTBF mean time between failures (reliability measured in flight hours)
MTI moving target indication (a radar facility)
NASA (US) National Aeronautics and Space Administration
NDB non-directional beacon (a navigation aid)

nm nautical mile (equal to 6080 ft. or 1854 metres)
OCU operational conversion unit (where a military pilot learns to fly the type of aircraft he is to operate)
OGE out of ground effect (ref helicopter performance)
P&W Pratt & Whitney
PFA (UK) Popular Flying Association
RAAF Royal Australian Air Force
RAE Royal Aircraft Establishment
RAeS Royal Aeronautical Society
RAF Royal Air Force
RFC Royal Flying Corps (part of the British Army prior to April 1918, that was the forerunner of the RAF)
RN Royal Navy
RPV remotely-piloted vehicle (ie, a radio-controlled drone)
R-R Rolls-Royce
SAC (USAF) Strategic Air Command
SAM surface-to-air missile
SAR search and rescue, or specific air range (ie, the distance flown per unit of fuel)
SFC specific fuel consumption (fuel flow rate per unit thrust)
shp shaft horse power
SLAR side-looking airborne radar
SST supersonic transport
STOL short take-off and landing
TAC (USAF) Tactical Air Command
TAS true airspeed (equals ground-speed under zero wind conditions)
TBO time between overhauls (eg, for an engine module)
t/c thickness/chord ratio (for an aerofoil section)
TFR terrain-following radar
T/O take-off
U/C undercarriage
UHF ultra-high frequency (radio)
USAF United States Air Force (formerly USAAF)
USAFE United States Air Forces in Europe
USMC United States Marine Corps
USN United States Navy
V_D maximum permitted dive speed
VFR visual flight rules
VHF very high frequency (radio)
V/STOL vertical or short take-off and landing
ZFW zero fuel weight (maximum aircraft weight without fuel)

Glossary

Aeroplane A powered, fixed wing aircraft.

Afterburner A device for augmenting the thrust of a turbojet or turbofan by burning extra fuel in the jetpipe.

Aileron A movable surface normally at the outer trailing end of the wing, providing roll control.

Aircraft Any type of vehicle intended for flight within the atmosphere, including balloons, airships and helicopters.

Air Defence The interception of intruding bombers and reconnaissance aircraft.

Air Superiority Control of the air, through the destruction of enemy fighters in dogfight actions.

Angle of Attack The inclination of the aerofoil to the direction of the airflow.

Angle of Incidence Strictly, the setting of the wing relative to the fuselage axis. Sometimes used in the UK to mean angle of attack.

Anhedral The downward angle of a wing in front-view.

Area Rule The lengthwise distribution of an aircraft's cross-section area to minimize wave drag.

Aspect Ratio The ratio of the wing span to average chord, which governs the drag caused by lift and the best glide angle.

Autogyro A rotary-wing aircraft with an unpowered rotor, with thrust normally provided by a propeller.

Bleed Air Gas extracted from a turbine engine to provide power or heat.

Blown Flap A wing flap with bleed air discharged over the upper surface to draw with it the surrounding flow, and thus prevent separations.

Bypass Ratio A term describing a turbofan engine, being the ratio of the air that bypasses the basic gas generator to the flow that goes through it. The higher the bypass, the more economical the engine.

Canard A foreplane, or an aircraft with a foreplane.

Chaff Strips of aluminium, dropped from an aircraft to produce spurious radar returns.

Chord The lengthwise dimension of an aerofoil.

Clean An aircraft with undercarriage and flaps retracted, or with no external stores.

Composites Materials produced by bonding together filaments of very high strength.

Convertible A transport aircraft which can be readily adapted to take either passengers or freight.

Course In aircraft navigation, the desired direction of travel.

Cruise Missile A long-range guided weapon, normally powered by a turbine engine and flying at very low level.

Derated An engine in which the maximum power is reduced in order to improve its life.

Dibber A bomb specifically designed to produce the maximum possible area of upheaval in a concrete runway.

Dihedral The upward inclination of a wing in front-view, used to generate a rolling movement in sideslip.

Disposable Load Payload/warload, plus fuel and crew.

Doppler Radar that exploits the frequency shift produced by the relative speed of the target, especially in detecting low-flying aircraft.

Elevator A movable surface on the trailing edge of the horizontal tail (or tailplane) providing pitch control on low-speed aircraft.

Foreplane A horizontal surface ahead of the main wing.

Glide Ratio A measure of sailplane efficiency, being the ratio of distance travelled to the height lost in still air.

Glove In a variable-sweep aircraft, the fixed inner portion of wing, into which the outer part slides.

▲ **A B-45 Tornado,** the USAF's first operational jet bomber.

Elevon A trailing edge surface on the wing of a tailless delta, providing both pitch and roll control.

Feathering Aligning the blades of a propeller with the direction of airflow to minimize drag with power off.

Fence A shallow vertical surface, normally attached to the upper skin of a wing to restrict the outward flow of the air close to the surface.

Fin The fixed part of the vertical tail.

Fly-by-Wire Electrically-signalled (as distinct from mechanically operated) controls.

Gross Area The area of wing that includes a notional part within the fuselage, produced by joining the root chords or by extending the leading- and trailing edges to the centre-line.

Heading In aircraft navigation, the direction in which the aircraft is pointed, which differs from its actual track because of crosswind.

Helicopter A rotary-wing aircraft with one or more powered rotors providing both lift and thrust.

Hydraulics Aircraft systems in which power is supplied to remote actuators (to move the undercarriage, flaps, etc) in the form of high-pressure oil.

181

Induced Drag Aerodynamic drag associated with wing lift.

▼ The Mystère IV.

Inertial Navigation Dead-reckoning navigation based on measurement of the aircraft's acceleration in north, east and vertical components, produced by sensors on a stabilized platform.

Integral Construction The manufacture as a single component of complex shapes such as aircraft skins and stiffeners, which would previously have been built by joining together separate parts.

Integral Tanks Fuel tanks produced by sealing parts of the aircraft structure rather than installing bag tanks.

Knot A speed of one nautical mile per hour.

Mach Number Aircraft speed relative to the speed of sound at the temperature of the surrounding air. Concorde flying at Mach 2·0 is flying at twice the speed of sound.

Navaid Navigation aid, such as NBD.

Payload Revenue-generating load, such as passengers, cargo and mail.

Pneumatics Aircraft systems in which power is supplied in the form of high-pressure air, usually from an engine-driven pump.

Port The left side, facing forwards.

Profile Drag The aerodynamic drag of an object at zero lift.

Radius The distance an aircraft can fly and then return to base without landing to refuel.

Range The distance an aircraft can fly on a one-way basis.

Root Where the wing joins the fuselage.

Rudder A movable surface at the trailing edge of the fin, providing control of yaw angle and sideslip.

Semi-active A form of missile guidance, in which the weapon homes on to radar energy transmitted by the launch aircraft and reflected by the target.

Service Ceiling The height at which the aircraft's best climb rate has fallen to a certain small value, such as 30·48 m/min (100 ft./min).

Servo Usually an actuator in the flying controls system.

Span The dimension of the wing from tip to tip.

Stall The start of flow separations from the upper surface of the wing, causing a loss of lift. This condition dictates the aircraft's minimum flying speed.

Starboard The right side, facing forwards.

Stick Pusher/Shaker A device that pushes forwards or merely shakes the control column or 'stick' to avoid or provide warning of a stall. This usually applies in the case of an aircraft with potentially dangerous handling characteristics or inadequate natural stall warning.

Store A fuel tank or armament carried externally.

Sweep Angle The rearward sweep of the wing when seen from above. For convenience, the angle is often given for the leading edge, but the value for the quarter-chord line is more meaningful.

Tailplane The principal horizontal surface. In high-performance aircraft, this is generally built as a single slab, and described in the US as a horizontal stabilizer or stabilator (ie combined stabilizer and elevator).

Thrust Vectoring The rotation of the jets between horizontal and vertical to provide V/STOL or improve manoevrability.

Track The path of the aircraft over the ground.

Trailing Edge The aft-facing edge of the wing.

Turbofan A gas turbine jet engine in which part of the airflow bypasses the core where combustion takes place. This provides improved propulsion efficiency, but thrust decreases with forward speed.

Turbojet The basic form of gas turbine engine, in which all the air flow passes through the compressor, combustion system and turbines.

Turboprop A gas turbine engine in which most of the thrust is produced by a separate turbine driving a propeller.

Turboshaft A gas turbine engine in which a separate turbine is used to extract power, usually to drive a helicopter's rotor.

▲ **A Harrier** takes off.

Variable Sweep The ability to change wing sweep angle in flight. This is done to reduce drag and gust response at high speeds (with maximum sweep) and to improve slow speed performance in the 'spread' position. Also described as variable geometry, or 'swing-wing'.

Warload The weight of guns, bombs, rockets, etc.

Wave Drag The aerodynamic drag associated with shock waves created by the aircraft flying at high speeds.

Winglet A vertical surface added to the wingtip, to reduce induced drag.

Zero-Zero A description applied to an ejection seat that can provide a safe escape, even at zero altitude and zero forward speed.

183

National Civil Aircraft Markings

Code	Country	Code	Country	Code	Country
AP	Pakistan	J6	St Lucia	VB	Brunei
A2	Botswana	J7	Dominica	XA/B/C	Mexico
A3	Tonga	J8	St Vincent	XT	Upper Volta
A5	Bhutan	LN	Norway	XU	Kampuchea
A6	United Arab	LV	Argentina	XY	Burma
	Emirates	LX	Luxembourg	YA	Afghanistan
A7	Qatar	LZ	Bulgaria	YI	Iraq
A9C	Bahrain	MI	Marshall Is.	YJ	Vanuatu
A40	Oman	N	USA	YK	Syria
B	China	OB	Peru	YN	Nicaragua
	(People's	OD	Lebanon	YR	Romania
	Repulic)	OE	Austria	YS	El Salvador
B	China/Taiwan	OH	Finland	YU	Yugoslavia
BNMAL	Mongolia	OK	Czechoslovakia	YV	Venezuela
C	Canada	OO	Belgium	Z	Zimbabwe
CC	Chile	OY	Denmark	ZA	Albania
CCCP	Soviet Union	P	Korea (DPRK)	ZK	New Zealand
CN	Morocco	PH	Netherlands	ZP	Paraguay
CP	Bolivia	PJ	Netherlands	ZS	South Africa
CR-C	Cape Verde Is.		Antilles	3A	Monaco
CS	Portugal	PK	Indonesia	3B	Mauritius
CU	Cuba	PP/PT	Brazil	3C	Equatorial
CX	Uruguay	PZ	Surinam		Guinea
C2	Nauru	P2	Papua New	3D	Swaziland
C5	Gambia		Guinea	3X	Guinea
C6	Bahamas	RDPL	Laos	4R	Sri Lanka
C9	Mozambique	RP	Philippines	4W	Yemen Arab
D	Federal	SE	Sweden		Republic
	Republic of	SP	Poland	4X	Israel
	Germany	ST	Sudan	5A	Libya
DDR	German	SU	Egypt	5B	Cyprus
	Democratic	SX	Greece	5H	Tanzania
	Republic	S2	Bangladesh	5N	Nigeria
DQ	Fiji	S7	Seychelles	5R	Madagascar
DZ	Angola	S9	Sao Tomé	5T	Mauritania
D6	Comoros Is.	TC	Turkey	5U	Niger
EC	Spain	TF	Iceland	5V	Togo
EI	Eire	TG	Guatemala	5W	Western
EL	Liberia	TI	Costa Rica		Samoa
EP	Iran	TJ	Cameroon	5X	Uganda
ET	Ethiopia	TL	Central African	5Y	Kenya
F	France		Republic	6O	Somalia
F-O	French Ov.	TN	Congo	6V	Senegal
	Depts/Pro-		Brazzaville	6Y	Jamaica
	tectorates	TR	Gabon	7O	People's Dem.
G	Great Britain	TS	Tunisia		Rep. of Yemen
HA	Hungary	TT	Chad	7P	Lesotho
HB	Switzerland &	TU	Ivory Coast	7Q	Malawi
	Liechtenstein	TY	Benin	7T	Algeria
HC	Ecuador	TZ	Mali	8P	Barbados
HH	Haiti	T3	Kinbati	8Q	Maldives
HI	Dominican Rep.	VH	Australia		Republic
HK	Colombia	VN	Vietnam	8R	Guyana
HL	Republic of	VP-F	Falkland Is.	9G	Ghana
	Korea	VP-LKA/LZ	St Kitts-Nevis	9H	Malta
HP	Panama	VP-LMA/LUZ	Montserrat	9J	Zambia
HR	Honduras	VP-LUA/ZZ	British Virgin Is.	9K	Kuwait
HS	Thailand	VQ-T	Turks & Cacos	9L	Sierra Leone
HZ	Saudi Arabia		Islands	9M	Malaysia
H4	Solomon Is.	VR-B	Bermuda	9N	Nepal
I	Italy	VR-C	Cayman Is.	9Q	Zaire
JA	Japan	VT-G	Gibraltar	9U	Burundi
JY	Jordan	VR-H	Hong Kong	9V	Singapore
J2	Djibouti	VT	India	9XR	Rwanda
J3	Grenada	V2	Antigua	9Y	Trinidad &
J5	Guinea Bissau	V3	Belize		Tobago

184

Index

187

ACKNOWLEDGEMENTS

8 Mansell Collection; 9 Messerschmitt-Bölkow Blohm GmbH; 10 Michael Holford; 12, 13, 18, 21, 22 Mansell Collection; 23 Courtesy National Film Archive; 24 left Mansell Collection, centre and right Popperfoto; 25 Mansell Collection; 28 Mansell Collection; 36 Embraer; 39 De Havilland Aircraft; 41 Boeing; 42 Kenneth Munson; 43 Courtesy Aerospatiale; 44 Messerschmitt-Bölkow Blohm GmbH; 46 Fairchild Republic Co; 48–49 MARS; 112 Embraer; 117 Embraer; 118 Union Syndicale des Industries Aeronautiques; 119 Bell Helicopters Textron; 121 Boeing; 181 Rockwell International; 182 Avions Marcel Dassault, Paris; 183 British Aerospace

Picture Research: Jackie S. Cookson